The Hamlyn
griddling
cookbook

The Hamlyn griddling cookbook

HAMLYN

First published in 1999 by Hamlyn
an imprint of Octopus Publishing Group Ltd
2-4 Heron Quays, London E14 4JB

British Cataloguing-in-Publication Data
A catalogue record for this book is available from the British Library

ISBN 0 600 596 70 2

Printed in China

Publishing Director: Laura Bamford

Commissioning Editor: Nicky Hill
Editors: Sharyn Conlan and Anne Crane

Creative Director: Keith Martin
Senior Designer: Geoff Fennell

Indexer: Hilary Bird
Nutritional analyst: Carol Bateman

Production Controller: Katherine Hockley

Recipes: Copyright © Octopus Publishing Group Ltd
with special thanks to Fran Warde and Becky Johnson

NOTES

- All the recipes in this book have been analysed by a professional nutritionist, so that you can see their nutritional content at a glance. The abbreviations are as follows:
  Kcal = calories
  KJ = kilojoules
  CHO = carbohydrate.
  The analysis refers to each portion

- Both metric and imperial measurements have been given in all recipes. Use one set of measurements only and not a mixture of both.

- Standard level spoon measurements are used in all recipes.
  1 tablespoon = one 15 ml spoon
  1 teaspoon = one 5 ml spoon

- Eggs should be medium to large unless otherwise stated.

- Milk should be full fat unless otherwise stated.

- Meat and poultry should be cooked thoroughly. To test if poultry is cooked, pierce the flesh through the thickest part with a skewer or fork – the juices should run clear, never pink or red. Do not re-freeze poultry that has been frozen previously and thawed.

- Do not re-freeze a dish that has been frozen previously.

- Pepper should be freshly ground black pepper unless otherwise stated.

- Fresh herbs should be used, unless otherwise stated. If unavailable, use dried herbs as an alternative but halve the quantities stated.

- Measurements for canned food have been given as a standard metric equivalent.

- Ovens should be preheated to the specified temperature – if using a fan-assisted oven, follow the manufacturer's instructions for adjusting the time and the temperature.

Contents

Introduction

 Griddling is one of the most popular cooking methods. It is not a new means of cooking as griddles were used as far back as biblical times and beyond. The word 'bakestone' (a term still used in Wales) was one of the most common names for a griddle plate, and provides us with the most direct clue to its origins. It refers to the timeless custom of cooking food on a large, flat, smooth stone, heated up over an open fire. This was almost certainly the ancestor of the more sophisticated griddling implements developed over later centuries. Traditional ways do not always disappear so easily however – heated stones are still used by various nomadic peoples to bake unleavened flat breads.

Metal griddles

With the discovery of iron and other useful metals, heavy, cast-iron griddle plates (commonly called girdles or bakestones) became universally popular for baking breads, scones and cakes over open fires and coal ranges. These griddles were usually flat and smooth without raised sides. In Celtic countries, such as Scotland, Ireland and Wales, cast-iron griddle plates were a familiar cooking implement in most households until relatively recently. Many people still consider this kind of griddle as the ideal piece of equipment for baking chapattis, and it is also perfect for baking oatcakes, Welsh cakes, girdle scones, buckwheat pancakes, and various other unleavened breads, scones or pancakes.

Why griddling?

More and more people are discovering the joy of griddling food. Griddling is a quick and easy method of indoor grilling using a ridged griddle pan. It is a more healthy method than frying or roasting and imparts distinctive and attractive markings to the food. Nowadays, excellent quality griddle pans are widely available, and are also conveniently designed for use with the most up-to-date stoves and cookers. Consequently, more people are discovering the delights and advantages of this fun, fast method of cooking. Cooking with a griddle pan is gratifyingly easy and produces sensational results. With a griddle pan, anyone can create a mouth-watering range of dishes that are imaginative, fresh, light, and positively filled with good flavour. Many modern griddling recipes consist of a repertoire of ingredients that are perfectly in tune with today's food trends – effortlessly blending elements from Eastern and Western cuisines and using a wide range of herbs and flavourings with style and flair. The sheer variety of dishes that can be cooked in a griddle pan is very appealing – the emphasis is on crisp vegetables, fresh fish, good quality poultry and game, and various kinds of meat. There are also scrumptious fruit and other dessert recipes.

Low fat option

Nowadays, many people prefer to use the minimum amount of fat in their cooking. A major benefit of griddling is that there is no need to use extra oil or fat in the cooking process. This is particularly true if you are using a griddle pan with a non-stick surface. Some people do prefer to brush or spray griddle pans that do not have a non-stick surface with a small amount of oil. This is helpful when griddling lean foods. Griddling is a very attractive cooking method for those who prefer a light, healthy, low-fat cooking approach. With this in mind, the recipes in this book have been created using the freshest, tastiest ingredients, and each dish has been nutritionally analysed.

Choosing a griddle pan

Griddling has become increasingly popular, and an enormous range of pans is now available. For the style conscious who like their cooking utensils colour co-ordinated, modern griddle pans are made in a delightful range of colours. Also, if you have a halogen hob, you can buy a special griddle pan for use on the extra-flat surface. In general however, the main thing to remember when purchasing a griddle pan is to buy the heaviest, best quality pan you can afford. This is because the pan needs to withstand high temperatures,

and cheap pans may distort and buckle. A typical griddle pan looks like a frying pan, with distinctive ridges across the surface. These ridges give food that appetizing, fresh-off-the-barbecue look. The shape of the pan may be round or square, and some pans have a lip on the side for pouring off juices or for draining off fat. Choose a small or large family-style griddle pan to suit your cooking lifestyle.

Principles of griddling

One of the best reasons to start griddling food is that following griddling recipes is truly easy and requires only minimum culinary skills. The basic method in griddling is to preheat the griddle pan so that the surface is very hot before starting to cook. Then the food is quickly seared on both sides to form a crust that will seal in the juices and lock in the flavours. It is important that this crust forms before the food is turned over to sear on the other side, otherwise it will stick to the pan. As soon as the food is seared on both sides, the heat is often lowered for the remaining cooking time, allowing the food to cook through. It might take a little practice to get this right at first, as the intensity of heat from different cookers can vary quite widely.

Caring for a griddle pan

Before using your griddle pan for the first time, wash it using hot soapy water. Manufacturers usually supply instructions on how to care for their griddle pans, so do take time to read these. It is worth while taking good care of your pan, so that it will give you many years of use. Always use plastic or wooden utensils on a griddle pan or it may become scratched. Good quality non-stick pans are easy to clean after use – simply wash the pan in warm, soapy water with a cloth or sponge and dry the surface thoroughly. Do not use scourers or abrasive cleaning materials, as these damage the non-stick surface. If your pan does not have a non-stick surface, fill it with soapy water immediately after cooking and leave it to soak. As with non-stick pans, avoid using abrasive materials – the cooking surface can still be damaged. You can brush the griddling surface with a light film of oil after washing and drying but it is not really necessary. Never run cold water over a hot griddle pan as it may cause warping.

Useful Equipment

Sharp knives – stainless steel are best. Keep them sharp and clean. They are invaluable for trimming and cutting pieces of meat and other ingredients into convenient shapes.

Tongs – are ideal for turning food after one side has been seared and cooked. Using tongs means that you avoid piercing the surface of meat with a fork, which would release the juices that need to be kept sealed inside by the cooking process.

Pastry brush – using a pastry brush makes it very easy to brush the surface of food with any glazes, pastes, sauces or marinades that may be used in a recipe.

Chopping board – invaluable for chopping herbs and other ingredients.

Pestle and mortar – perfect for grinding fresh peppercorns and other seeds and spices.

Herbs and Flavourings

Fresh herbs are frequently used throughout this book. They add superb, piquant flavour and colour to food. Chives, oregano, basil, coriander, thyme and rosemary are often used in generous quantities, so unless you are lucky enough to have a large herb garden, you will need to buy these. Fortunately, most large supermarkets sell packets or growing pots of fresh herbs, and many grocers offer large bunches of flat-leaf parsley (which has more flavour than the curly variety) and fresh coriander. Herbs are either seared with the main ingredients, added to salad dressings, or simply arranged with the food as a garnish.

Other flavoursome ingredients that play an important part in the recipes include toasted pine nuts, olives, garlic, chillies and freshly grated Parmesan and pecorino cheeses.

Marinades and Sauces

Certain types of meat and fish benefit greatly from being marinated before cooking. Marinades can be as simple as a little olive oil with a splash of lemon juice, perhaps with a little added yogurt, or they may be more heavily flavoured with garlic, honey, chillies or other spices. There are a wide range of sauces which can be served with griddled meats, many of which can be purchased ready-made if time is short. Before griddling, brush off any marinade ingredients such as chopped onion or garlic as they will burn and stick to the pan if left on.

Barbecue Sauce – complements steaks, chops, sausages and chicken pieces.

Salsas – make a fresh and spicy addition to chicken, game and meat.

Yogurt – flavoured with chives, mint, lemon, spices or cucumber is delicious served with griddled chicken or lamb.

Herb butters

These butters make great toppings for your griddled fish, meat and vegetable dishes. It is best to use butter which is cool and firm, but not taken straight out of the refrigerator.

Basil Butter

75 g/3 oz butter
1 garlic clove, peeled
2 tablespoons chopped basil
1 tablespoon lemon juice
salt and pepper

1 Blend the butter in a food processor or blender, adding the remaining ingredients. Chill until firm.

2 Alternatively, pound the butter in a mortar until it is creamy, then add the remaining ingredients gradually until they are well mixed. Chill until firm.

Variations

Parsley Butter: use the same method with 3 tablespoons chopped parsley.

Mint Butter: use the same method with 2 tablespoons chopped mint.

Chive Butter: omit the garlic and use the same method with 2 tablespoons chopped chives.

Oils and dressings

Olive oil is the oil most commonly used throughout the *Hamlyn Griddling Cookbook*. Buy the best quality that you can afford, and don't be afraid to try out the various other kinds of oils. These include sunflower, safflower, sesame seed, walnut, hazelnut, groundnut, pumpkin seed and grapeseed. Grapeseed oil is useful to mix with stronger oils if you want to soften the flavour. Experiment with different oils to discover which ones you like best.
Making your own flavoured oils and dressings will please your taste buds and is more economical than buying the expensive versions sold in shops. There is also a wonderful recipe for Lemon Oil (see page 91).

Lime and Sesame Dressing

50 ml/2 fl oz sesame oil

25 ml/1 fl oz sunflower oil

2 tablespoons lime juice

pinch of sugar

salt and pepper

1 Put all the ingredients in a screw-top jar and shake vigorously to emulsify.

Tarragon Oil

4 tablespoons chopped tarragon

450 ml/¾ pint olive oil (or other oil)

1 Pound the tarragon briefly in a mortar with a pestle. Add a little of the oil and pound again. Gradually add the rest of the oil then pour into a wide-mouthed glass bottle. Seal tightly.

2 Keep the oil for 2 weeks before using, shaking the bottle every 2 or 3 days.

Fragrant Oil

450 ml/¾ pint olive oil (or other oil)

2 sprigs of rosemary

6 sprigs of thyme

1 large garlic clove, peeled and halved

1 green chilli pepper

5–6 small red chillies

6 black peppercorns

6 juniper berries

1 Pour the oil into a clear glass bottle which has a tightly fitting cork. Wash the herbs thoroughly and dry with kitchen paper. Put the herbs into the oil with the remaining ingredients. Seal tightly.

2 Keep the oil for 2 weeks before using, shaking the bottle every 2 or 3 days.

Variations

Instead of using whole sprigs of rosemary, thyme, or tarragon, chop the herbs before you put them in the oil. They will flavour the oil and look attractive as well. You can also make a spicy chilli oil by gently heating some olive oil with a few dried chillies and leaving it to infuse overnight. Strain the oil the next day and transfer it to a clear glass bottle with a tight fitting cork.

vegetables

Crisp, fresh vegetables and many firm-textured cheeses can be creatively combined to make healthy and delicious starters, side dishes and main courses.

potato wedges
with sun-dried tomato aïoli

Serves	**4**
Preparation time	**15–20** minutes
Cooking time	**20–55** minutes
Kcal	**766**
KJ	**3166**
Protein	**5** g
Fat	**72** g
CHO	**27** g

4 large potatoes

4 tablespoons olive oil

paprika

sea salt and pepper

sun-dried tomato aïoli:

4–6 garlic cloves, crushed

2 egg yolks

juice ½ lemon, plus extra to taste

300 ml/½ pint extra virgin olive oil

**8 sun-dried tomato halves in oil,
    drained and finely chopped**

1 If using wooden skewers, soak them in cold water for 30 minutes.

2 Place the whole, unpeeled potatoes in a large pan of cold water, bring to the boil, then reduce the heat and simmer for 15–20 minutes or until just tender. Drain, and when they are cool enough to handle, cut each potato into large wedges.

3 To make the sun-dried tomato aïoli, place the garlic and egg yolks in a food processor or blender, add the lemon juice and process briefly to mix. With the motor running, gradually add the oil in a thin stream until the mixture forms a thick cream. Scrape into a bowl and stir in the sun-dried tomatoes, season with salt and pepper, adding more lemon juice if liked.

4 Brush the potato wedges with the oil, sprinkle with a little paprika. Skewer or lay the potato wedges on a heated griddle pan and cook for 5–6 minutes, turning them frequently until golden brown. Serve with the aïoli.

Aïoli is a tasty mayonnaise-like sauce made with olive oil, egg yolks and garlic. It originated in Provence.

sweet potato chips

4	Serves
15 minutes	Preparation time
about **30** minutes	Cooking time
210	Kcal
890	KJ
5 g	Protein
4 g	Fat
41 g	CHO

1 Cut the sweet potato into slices 2.5 cm/1 inch wide, then cut the slices into 2.5 cm/1 inch chips. Heat the griddle pan and add a single layer of chips, leaving a little room between each one. Cook for about 3 minutes on each side, or 12 minutes in total. Remove from the griddle and keep warm. Repeat until all the sweet potato is cooked. Sprinkle the chips with sea salt and pepper and arrange on a large platter, with room for a dipping bowl.

750 g/1½ lb sweet potatoes, peeled

sea salt and pepper

dip:

150 g/5 oz strained natural yogurt

1 shallot, finely diced

1 small red chilli, deseeded and
    finely diced

bunch of coriander, chopped

few drops of Tabasco sauce

2 To make the dip, mix the yogurt, shallot, chilli, coriander, Tabasco and salt and pepper, to taste in a small bowl. Serve on the same plate as the sweet potato.

Sweet potatoes come in several varieties; the flesh can vary from almost white to deep yellow in colour. They are used in exactly the same way as ordinary potatoes – griddled, roasted, mashed, fried or boiled.

naan vegetable

sandwich

Serves	**4**
Preparation time	**10** minutes
Cooking time	**30** minutes
Kcal	**247**
KJ	**1035**
Protein	**9** g
Fat	**11** g
CHO	**30** g

1 Have all the vegetables, sliced and griddled in advance.

2 Heat the griddle pan, cut the naan into 4 portions, slice each one in half and griddle the soft side for 2 minutes or until toasted. Rub with garlic and spoon a little oil over each toasted side.

2 peppers, griddled

1 small aubergine, griddled

2 courgettes, griddled

4 flat mushrooms, griddled

1 oak leaf lettuce, washed

1 naan bread

2 garlic cloves

1 tablespoon olive oil

1 tablespoon water

3 tablespoons fromage frais

1 tablespoon chopped parsley

sea salt and pepper

3 Mix the water, fromage frais and parsley together, and season with salt and pepper.

4 Place the peppers, aubergine, courgettes, mushrooms and lettuce on the bread, and season with salt and pepper. Spoon over the thinned fromage frais and top with a second piece of naan.

Great variations can be made on this sandwich, adding cheese, bacon, griddled fish or chicken, and different dressings can also be used. The cheese and pickle sandwich will be a thing of the past!

aubergine, haloumi
and cumin bruschetta

4	Serves
5 minutes, plus infusing time	Preparation time
18–30 minutes	Cooking time
405	Kcal
1692	KJ
17 g	Protein
29 g	Fat
21 g	CHO

1 tablespoon cumin seeds

4 tablespoons extra virgin olive oil,
   plus extra for drizzling

grated rind of 1 lemon

2 small aubergines, each cut
   lengthways into 4 slices

4 thick slices of day-old country
   bread

250 g/8 oz haloumi, cut into
   4 slices

2 garlic cloves, cut in half

125 g/4 oz rocket leaves

1 Dry roast the cumin seeds in a small frying pan until they start to pop and give off a smoky aroma. Add the oil and lemon rind, remove from the heat and leave to infuse for several hours.

2 Heat the griddle pan and cook the aubergine slices for 4–5 minutes on each side. Remove from the pan and dip each slice into the cumin-scented oil, reserving the remaining oil. Spread out the aubergine slices on a plate and cool to room temperature.

3 Just before serving, prepare the bruschetta. Heat the griddle pan, add the slices of bread and toast each side. Add the haloumi and cook on each side for 1–2 minutes, turning it carefully with a palette knife or spatula. Rub the toast all over with the cut garlic halves and drizzle with olive oil. Toss the rocket in the remaining cumin oil and heap on top of the bruschetta. Arrange slices of aubergine and haloumi on top and serve immediately.

Haloumi is a semi-hard cheese from Greece and Cyprus. It has an elastic texture and a creamy, slightly salty taste, making it a perfect cheese for griddling.

mixed onion
and tagliatelle with pecorino

Serves	**4**
Preparation time	**10** minutes
Cooking time	**30** minutes
Kcal	**863**
KJ	**3625**
Protein	**36** g
Fat	**35** g
CHO	**107** g

4 small leeks, cut into large chunks

4 spring onions

2 red onions, cut into wedges but
   root left intact

1 white onion, cut into wedges but
   root left intact

2 shallots, cut into wedges but root
   left intact

4 garlic cloves, sliced

500 g/1 lb fresh tagliatelle

150 ml/¼ pint double cream

175 g/6 oz pecorino cheese,
   coarsely grated

bunch of chives, chopped

sea salt and pepper

1 Heat the griddle pan, add the leeks and cook for 6 minutes, turning constantly. Transfer to a shallow baking dish and place in a preheated oven, 180°C (350°F), Gas Mark 4, to continue to soften. Repeat the process with the spring onions, cooking them for 4 minutes, then add to the leeks in the oven.

2 Cook the onions and shallots on the griddle for 3–6 minutes, depending on size, then transfer to the oven with the leeks and spring onions. Quickly griddle the garlic slices for 1 minute on each side, then remove them and set aside. Continue to cook the onion mixture in the oven for a further 10 minutes.

3 Heat a large pan of boiling water, stir in the pasta and cook for 3 minutes, or until *al dente*. Drain well, then return to the pan. Add the onion mixture, garlic, cream, cheese and chives, and season with salt and pepper. Toss well and serve immediately.

Include every member of the onion family available, griddle them and mix with soft, velvety fresh pasta. The result is sensational.

sweetcorn fritters
with mustard crème fraîche

4	Serves
10 minutes	Preparation time
about **20** minutes	Cooking time
474	Kcal
198	KJ
25 g	Protein
26 g	Fat
38 g	CHO

2 tablespoons plain flour

1 tablespoon self-raising flour

1 large egg, beaten

375 g/12 oz fresh, frozen or canned
  sweetcorn

2 tablespoons chopped spring
  onions

1 garlic clove, crushed

2 sticks celery, finely chopped

200 g/7 oz grated Mozzarella
  cheese

8 thin slices of Parma ham

a little oil, for brushing

sea salt and pepper

dill sprigs, to garnish

mustard crème fraîche:

2 tablespoons wholegrain mustard

100 ml/3½ fl oz crème fraîche

1 Sift the flours into a bowl, make a well in the centre and add the beaten egg. Whisk to make a thick batter.

2 Mix in the sweetcorn, spring onions, garlic, celery and grated mozzarella, adding a little water if necessary, but keeping the mixture very thick. Season to taste with salt and pepper.

3 Heat the griddle pan and brush with a little oil. Carefully drop spoonfuls of the sweetcorn mixture on to it. Flatten each fritter gently with a fish slice and griddle on both sides for 3–4 minutes until cooked through and golden brown in colour. Cook the remaining fritters the same way.

4 Mix the mustard and crème fraîche together in a bowl. Top each fritter with a slice of Parma ham and a large dollop of mustard crème fraîche. Garnish with dill.

hot asparagus
with balsamic vinegar dressing

Serves	**4**
Preparation time	**15** minutes
Cooking time	**5** minutes
Kcal	**146**
KJ	**600**
Protein	**8** g
Fat	**11** g
CHO	**3** g

500 g/1 lb young asparagus spears, trimmed

50 g/2 oz pine nuts, toasted

25 g/1 oz Parmesan cheese, shaved into thin slivers

sea salt and pepper

1 To make the dressing, mix the balsamic vinegar, garlic, tomatoes and olive oil in a bowl and reserve.

2 Heat the griddle pan, add the asparagus in a single layer and cook for 5 minutes on a medium heat, turning constantly.

balsamic vinegar dressing:

2 tablespoons balsamic vinegar

1–2 garlic cloves, crushed

375 g/12 oz tomatoes, skinned, deseeded and chopped

5 tablespoons olive oil

3 Divide the asparagus between 4 warmed plates. Spoon over the balsamic vinegar dressing, top with the pine nuts and Parmesan slivers and sprinkle with sea salt and pepper. Serve at once.

This is a very simple yet delicious way of serving young asparagus.

peppers
with goats' cheese and chilli relish

4	Serves
20 minutes	Preparation time
12–25 minutes	Cooking time
209	Kcal
869	KJ
9 g	Protein
15 g	Fat
10 g	CHO

2 red peppers

2 yellow peppers

2 individual goats' cheeses

1 tablespoon fresh thyme leaves

2 tablespoons extra virgin olive oil

25 g/1 oz pitted black olives, finely
    chopped

cracked black pepper

chilli relish:

6 large red chillies

2 tablespoons lime juice

2 garlic cloves, crushed

3 tablespoons chopped fresh flat
    leaf parsley or coriander

sea salt

1 First make the chilli relish. Heat the griddle pan, add the chillies and cook for about 5–10 minutes, turning occasionally until well charred and blistered all over. Place the chillies in a plastic bag and tie the top, leave to cool. When cool enough to handle, remove the stalks, cut the chillies in half and remove the seeds. Roughly chop the flesh.

2 Place the chillies in a mortar and pound with a pestle. Stir in the remaining ingredients and season with salt. Set aside.

3 Cut the peppers in half lengthways and remove the seeds. Leave the stalks attached but trim away any membrane. Heat the griddle pan, add the peppers and cook for 4 minutes on each side until well charred.

4 Cut each goats' cheese into 4 slices. Turn the peppers over, place a slice of goats' cheese in the centre, sprinkle with the thyme and olive oil and leave to cook for a further 10 minutes or until the peppers have softened and the goats' cheese has melted.

5 Sprinkle the peppers with the black olives and black pepper and serve with the chilli relish.

Take care when preparing chillies, never to let any part of the chilli go near your eyes. Always wash your hands, knives and chopping board after preparation.

potatoes
wrapped in prosciutto

Serves	**4**
Preparation time	**15** minutes
Cooking time	**10** minutes
Kcal	**110**
KJ	**470**
Protein	**6** g
Fat	**1** g
CHO	**19** g

12 new potatoes, cooked unpeeled

12 long, thin slices of prosciutto

sea salt and pepper

1 Wrap each of the potatoes in a slice of the prosciutto.

2 Heat the griddle pan, add the wrapped potatoes and cook on all sides for about 8 minutes, until the prosciutto is golden coloured and crunchy. Serve sprinkled with sea salt and pepper.

Griddled prosciutto turns a lovely golden colour and becomes moreishly crunchy. A good alternative to prosciutto is very thinly sliced bacon, which works well and costs less. These potatoes make a tasty accompaniment to griddled fish.

potato chips
with blue cheese dip

4	Serves
10 minutes	Preparation time
10 minutes	Cooking time
347	Kcal
1449	KJ
15 g	Protein
18 g	Fat
33 g	CHO

1 Heat the griddle pan. Slice the potatoes into approximately 1.5 cm/¾ inch slices, and cut in half lengthways to make big chips. Place on the griddle pan in batches and cook for 5 minutes on each side. When cooked, keep them warm and repeat until all the potatoes are done.

750 g/1½ lb baking potatoes
150 g/5 oz blue cheese, such as
   Stilton, Dolcelatte or Gorgonzola
4 tablespoons natural yogurt
sea salt and pepper

2 Using a fork or blender, mix together the blue cheese and yogurt until smooth. Season with pepper and transfer to a small dipping bowl.

3 Arrange the potatoes on a plate, sprinkle with salt and serve with the blue cheese dip.

These griddled potatoes are great served on their own, accompanied by a glass of wine before dinner. They are also delicious served with fish.

butternut squash
and parmesan

Serves	**4**
Preparation time	**10** minutes
Cooking time	**35** minutes
Kcal	**34**
KJ	**1411**
Protein	**17** g
Fat	**28** g
CHO	**69** g

1 Heat the griddle pan, add the squash in batches and cook for about 10 minutes on each side. As the squash wedges are cooked, place on a large plate and keep warm.

1 kg/2 lb butternut squash, deseeded and cut into small wedges or slices
75 g/3 oz butter
150 g/5 oz Parmesan cheese
sea salt and pepper

2 Melt the butter in a small pan and heat until it just begins to brown (which will give it a rich, nutty flavour). Pour the butter over the cooked squash and season with salt and pepper. Using a vegetable peeler, shave the Parmesan directly over the squash. Serve hot, or just warm (but before the butter hardens).

Squash is a great accompaniment to roasts, especially chicken, and children love it for its sweetness. The butternut can be bought all year round and keeps well in a cool place.

autumn vegetables
with garlic sauce

4	Serves
10 minutes	Preparation time
20 minutes	Cooking time
570	Kcal
3375	KJ
8 g	Protein
40 g	Fat
48 g	CHO

1 Blanch the garlic bulb for the garlic sauce in boiling water for 5 minutes. Drain and pat dry on kitchen paper.

2 Heat the griddle pan. Place a layer of vegetables on the pan and cook on all sides until soft. Make sure not to over-char the outsides, turning down the heat if needed. When the first batch is cooked, remove and keep warm, and add more vegetables to the griddle. Continue until all the vegetables are cooked. Toss the vegetables in the olive oil, adding salt and pepper to taste. Keep warm.

2 large onions, cut into wedges

5 small carrots, quartered

4 small parsnips

8 small potatoes, halved

2 fennel bulbs, sliced thickly

4 rosemary sprigs

4 thyme sprigs

4 tablespoons extra virgin olive oil

sea salt and pepper

garlic sauce:

1 large garlic bulb

1 large slice day-old bread, crusts removed

4 tablespoons milk

150 ml/¼ pint extra virgin olive oil

3 To make the garlic sauce, soak the bread slice in the milk for 5 minutes. Divide the blanched garlic bulb into cloves. Peel the cloves, and mash the flesh. Place the garlic and bread in a food processor or blender and process to form a smooth paste. Gradually blend in the olive oil, until combined. Season to taste.

4 To serve, arrange the vegetables on a platter and serve the garlic sauce separately.

vegetable brochettes

with mustard and herb glaze

Serves	**4**
Preparation time	**20** minutes, plus marinating
Cooking time	about **10–15** minutes
Kcal	**100**
KJ	**426**
Protein	**4** g
Fat	**2** g
CHO	**19** g

12 pickling onions

1 large red, green or yellow pepper

**2 or 3 vegetables, such as
   aubergines, courgettes, corn-on-
   the-cob or fennel bulbs**

24 button mushrooms

mustard and herb glaze:

2 tablespoons Dijon mustard

**2 tablespoons finely chopped
   mixed herbs (e.g. parsley, thyme,
   marjoram, basil)**

2 garlic cloves, crushed

4 tablespoons red wine vinegar

½–1 teaspoon sweet chilli sauce

2 teaspoons clear honey

salt and pepper

1 Plunge the pickling onions into boiling water and blanch for 2–3 minutes. Refresh under cold water, drain and peel. Cut the pepper in half lengthways, remove the seeds and cut the flesh into 2.5 cm/1 inch wedges. Slice the aubergines into 5 mm/¼ inch rounds. Cut the courgettes into 1.5 cm/¾ inch rounds and blanch for 1 minute. Cut the corn-on-the-cob into 1 cm/½ inch rounds and cook in boiling water for 2–3 minutes. Refresh and drain. Trim the fennel at the root to free the leaves and cut each bulb into 2.5 cm/1 inch pieces.

2 Arrange the vegetables in bowls on a tray. If using wooden skewers, soak them in cold water. Place a mushroom or onion at the end of each skewer to anchor the other vegetables, then thread an assortment of vegetables on each skewer to make a colourful display. Put the prepared brochettes on the tray.

3 Combine all the ingredients for the glaze in a bowl. Brush this generously over the brochettes, turning them so they are well coated. Cover with clingfilm and leave to marinate in the refrigerator until required, along with the remaining glaze.

4 Heat a griddle pan and add the brochettes. Griddle for about 10–15 minutes, turning to cook evenly. Serve with a salad and warm bread, if liked.

Brochette is the French name for the special type of skewer which is similar to a kebab. These brochettes can be made a couple of hours in advance.

mixed vegetables
with basil dressing

4	Serves
15 minutes	Preparation time
30 minutes	Cooking time
175	Kcal
738	KJ
8 g	Protein
5 g	Fat
27 g	CHO

2 red peppers

1 red onion, cut in 1 cm/½ inch
   slices

1 aubergine, cut in 1 cm/½ inch
   slices

2 courgettes, cut diagonally in
   1 cm/½ inch slices

sea salt and pepper

basil leaves, to garnish

basil dressing:

large bunch of basil

1 garlic clove, crushed

6 tablespoons olive oil

2 tablespoons white wine vinegar

1 Slice the bottom off each pepper, then slice down to give 4–5 flat, wide slices, leaving the seeds still attached to the core.

2 Heat the griddle pan and cook the onions for 3 minutes on each side, peppers for 4 minutes on each side, aubergine for 3 minutes on each side and the courgettes for 2 minutes on each side. As the vegetables cook, arrange them on a large platter.

3 To make the dressing, place all the ingredients in a small blender and process, or use a hand-held blender. Alternatively, chop the garlic and basil finely, place in a screw-top jar with the olive oil and vinegar and shake well to combine thoroughly.

4 Sprinkle the cooked vegetables with sea salt and pepper. Drizzle over the basil dressing and garnish with fresh basil leaves.

Vary the colours by using yellow or orange peppers and yellow courgettes and white onion or shallots.

griddled vegetables
with savoury salsa

Serves	**4**
Preparation time	**15** minutes, plus infusing
Cooking time	about **20** minutes
Kcal	**342**
KJ	**1411**
Protein	**3** g
Fat	**31** g
CHO	**13** g

4 garlic cloves, finely chopped

10–12 tablespoons extra virgin olive oil

1 large red onion, peeled and sliced into rings

4 mini fennel bulbs, or 1 small fennel bulb

2 large peppers (1 red, 1 yellow)

4 mini aubergines, or 2 small aubergines

4 baby courgettes, or 2 small courgettes

1 head chicory

4 large field mushrooms

Savoury Salsa (see page 120), to serve

to garnish:

1 large lemon, cut into wedges

flat leaf parsley sprigs

1 Put the garlic and olive oil in a bowl and leave to infuse while preparing the vegetables.

2 Place the onion rings on a large plastic or metal tray. Slice the small fennel bulb through its length into about 3 flat slices or leave mini fennel whole.

3 Cut the peppers in half lengthways deseed and remove the white membranes and stalks. Cut in half again. Place the pepper wedges on the tray. Slice the aubergines in half lengthways through the stalk if mini or small; if large, slice thinly from stalk to tip. With a sharp knife, lightly score the flesh of the aubergines in a criss-cross fashion. Set beside the peppers. Top and tail the courgettes and cut in half lengthways. Set on the tray.

4 Cut the chicory in half lengthways. Peel and remove the stalks from the mushrooms. Set on the tray. Brush each vegetable with the garlic-flavoured oil.

5 Add the vegetables which take longest to the griddle pan, gradually adding the rest until they are all cooked – onions and fennel take 10–15 minutes, peppers, aubergines and courgettes about 10 minutes, chicory and mushrooms 5 minutes. Turn the vegetables during cooking.

6 Arrange the vegetables on a large platter or individual plates and garnish with lemon and parsley. Serve with Savoury Salsa (see page 120) and crusty bread.

Griddled vegetables can also be served with salad leaves, drizzled with olive oil, seasoned with pepper and scattered with Parmesan shavings – this makes an excellent light lunch or first course.

tomato and olive
bruschetta

4	Serves
15 minutes, plus marinating	Preparation time
about **5** minutes	Cooking time
193	Kcal
805	KJ
4 g	Protein
12 g	Fat
18 g	CHO

1 Finely chop 1 garlic clove and put it in a bowl with the tomatoes, black and green olives, sun-dried tomatoes, half of the oil and the vinegar. Season with salt and pepper, to taste and add half of the parsley. Toss very gently to combine and leave to marinate for 10–15 minutes.

2 large garlic cloves, peeled

8–10 baby tomatoes, cut into thin slices

8 black olives, pitted and roughly chopped

8 green olives, pitted and roughly chopped

2 sun-dried tomatoes in oil, drained and roughly chopped

40 ml/1½ fl oz extra virgin olive oil

1 teaspoon balsamic vinegar

2 tablespoons finely chopped flat leaf parsley

4 slices of bread

4–8 basil leaves, torn into pieces

sea salt and pepper

2 Heat a griddle pan. Griddle the bread for 2 minutes on both sides. Cut the remaining garlic clove in half, then lightly rub each side of the toast with the cut sides of the garlic. Brush with the remaining oil and arrange the bread on a plate, Spoon the tomato and olive mixture on top. Sprinkle with the remaining parsley and the basil leaves, then drizzle with a little of the remaining oil. Serve warm.

Bruschetta are an excellent way of using up bread which is past its best but not yet stale. It can be served plain, or as a base for an infinite variety of toppings, such as salsa, tapenade, pesto and grilled goats' cheese.

polenta
with field mushrooms

Serves	**4**
Preparation time	**35** minutes, plus cooling
Cooking time	**20** minutes
Kcal	**34**
KJ	**1411**
Protein	**17** g
Fat	**28** g
CHO	**69** g

1 litre/1¾ pints boiling water

250 g/8 oz polenta flour

1 tablespoon olive oil

50 g/2 oz butter

375 g/12 oz field mushrooms,
  sliced

2 garlic cloves , crushed and
  chopped

bunch of thyme, chopped

2 tablespoons white wine

250 g/8 oz Parmesan cheese,
  shaved into slivers

sea salt and pepper

1 Bring the water to the boil in a large saucepan, add the polenta, season, and mix well until smooth. Turn the heat down and continue to mix for about 5 minutes until the polenta thickens and the water has been absorbed. The mixture will become very thick and hard to work. Using a spatula, spread the polenta out on a chopping board, or in an oiled 23 cm/9 inch springform cake tin. Leave to cool for about 1 hour.

2 Heat the oil and butter in a small saucepan, add the mushrooms, garlic and thyme, and cook for 8 minutes, until soft and dark. Add the white wine and simmer for 2 minutes, then season. Remove from the heat and keep warm.

3 Heat the griddle pan, cut the polenta into slices or wedges, and griddle on each side for about 4 minutes. Serve the griddled polenta with the mushroom mix spooned over one side and sprinkled with Parmesan shavings.

Griddled polenta is a very fashionable ingredient. The key to serving it perfectly is not to serve too much of it and to have a tasty vegetable to go with it, such as these field mushrooms.

linguine
with griddled vegetables

4	Serves
10 minutes	Preparation time
10 minutes	Cooking time
726	Kcal
3050	KJ
31 g	Protein
27 g	Fat
90 g	CHO

1 Heat the griddle pan then add the peppers, skin side down, and griddle until the skin blisters and blackens. Griddle the courgette, onion and aubergine slices and the asparagus for 2 minutes on each side.

2 Place a large saucepan of water on to boil for the pasta.

3 Peel the skin off the pepper and slice into ribbons. Place in a dish with the courgettes, onion, aubergine and asparagus, drizzle with olive oil and put in to a warm oven to keep warm.

4 Place the pasta in the boiling water and cook for 3–4 minutes if fresh and 8 minutes if dried, or according to packet instructions. Test a piece before draining. Add the petits pois for the last minute of the cooking time.

5 Drain the pasta and petits pois in a colander then return to the saucepan. Add the warm vegetables, season with salt and pepper and add the Parmesan. Toss will, using two spoons, adding a little more olive oil if necessary. Finally add the torn basil leaves and toss again, then serve immediately.

1 red pepper, cored, deseeded and
  cut into large squares

1 courgette, sliced

1 red onion, sliced

1 small aubergine, sliced into thin
  rounds

8 asparagus spears, trimmed

5 tablespoons olive oil

125 g/4 oz Parmesan cheese,
  freshly grated

500 g/1 lb linguine

handful of basil leaves,
  roughly torn

sea salt and pepper

griddled vegetable
and cheddar sandwich

Serves	**4**
Preparation time	**10** minutes
Cooking time	**10** minutes
Kcal	**617**
KJ	**2589**
Protein	**23** g
Fat	**29** g
CHO	**71** g

1 Heat the griddle pan. Cook all the vegetables for 5 minutes on each side.

2 Cut the French stick into 4 pieces, cut each piece in half and lightly toast the inside of the bread. Spread the mayonnaise all over the toasted side .

2 yellow peppers, sliced

1 red onion, sliced

2 courgettes, sliced

1 French stick

2 tablespoons mayonnaise

150 g/5 oz mature Cheddar, grated

1 bunch of wild rocket

sea salt and pepper

3 Arrange the griddled vegetables, cheese and rocket in the bread. Season to taste with salt and pepper.

4 Wrap with napkins to hold the sandwiches together and serve.

Quick and easy to prepare, this makes a delicious lunch. You could substitute mozzarella cheese for the Cheddar and basil for the rocket.

aubergine, tomato
and mozzarella towers

4	Serves
10 minutes	Preparation time
15–20 minutes	Cooking time
315	Kcal
1311	KJ
19 g	Protein
24 g	Fat
6 g	CHO

1 To make the pesto, put the garlic, basil, pine nuts and Parmesan in a food processor or blender and purée. Add the oil and blend again. Set aside.

1 aubergine, cut into 8 slices

4 beef tomatoes, skinned, then cut into 8 slices

250 g/8 oz packet buffalo mozzarella, cut into 8 slices

2 tablespoons olive oil

salt and pepper

mint sprigs, to garnish

pesto:

3 garlic cloves, crushed

handful of basil leaves

2 tablespoons pine nuts

50 g/2 oz Parmesan cheese, finely grated

3 tablespons olive oil

2 Heat the griddle pan, arrange the aubergine slices in the hot griddle pan and cook until browned on both sides.

3 To prepare the stacks, place 4 of the aubergine slices on a lightly oiled baking sheet. Put a tomato slice and a mozzarella slice on each one, then make a second layer of aubergine, tomato and mozzarella, sprinkling each layer with salt and pepper as you go. Skewer with a wooden cocktail stick through the centre to hold the stacks together.

4 Place the stacks in a preheated oven, 190°C (375°F), Gas Mark 5, and cook for 10 minutes.

5 Transfer the stacks to serving plates and remove the sticks. Drizzle with olive oil and top with the pesto. Garnish with mint sprigs and serve.

Serve with crusty Italian bread to mop up the pesto juices. If preparation time is really short, use ready-made pesto.

red lentil cakes

Serves	**makes 12 small burgers (enough for 6) per portion**
Preparation time	**30** minutes
Cooking time	about **35–55** minutes
Kcal	**478**
KJ	**2009**
Protein	**23** g
Fat	**22** g
CHO	**51** g

275 g/9 oz split red lentils

750 ml/1¼ pints boiling water

3 tablespoons sunflower oil

1 large onion, finely chopped

2–3 garlic cloves, finely chopped

65 g/2½ oz red pepper, deseeded
    and finely chopped

1–2 small red chillies, deseeded
    and finely chopped

250 g/8 oz fresh white
    breadcrumbs

150 g/5 oz mature Cheddar cheese,
    grated

1 tablespoon tomato purée

3 tablespoons finely chopped
    parsley

½ teaspoon yeast extract

1 small egg, beaten

salt and pepper

1 Wash the lentils and put them into a large saucepan of boiling water. Return to the boil, then reduce the heat to a simmer. Cook gently, stirring constantly, for 20–40 minutes until the lentils are pulpy, the liquid has evaporated and the mixture is dry in texture. Spread the lentils on a baking sheet and set aside to cool.

2 Meanwhile, heat a griddle pan. Heat the sunflower oil and griddle the onion, garlic, red pepper and chilli until soft but not coloured. Set aside to cool.

3 In a large bowl, combine the lentils, onion mixture, 150 g/5 oz of the breadcrumbs, the Cheddar, tomato purée, parsley and yeast extract. Stir well, season to taste with salt and pepper and add the beaten egg, then mix to combine.

4 Divide the mixture into 12 pieces. Dip them in the remaining breadcrumbs and make into cakes about 7 cm/3 inches in diameter. Heat the griddle pan, put on the prepared cakes and cook for about 5 minutes on each side. Serve hot.

Among the vegetable cook's great resources are lentils. They are inexpensive, versatile and nutritious, rich in protein, carbohydrates, vitamins and iron.

griddled asparagus

1	Serves
5 minutes	Preparation time
5–8 minutes	Cooking time
344	Kcal
1415	KJ
3 g	Protein
36 g	Fat
2 g	CHO

1 Melt the butter with the oil in a small saucepan over a low heat. Heat the griddle pan, add the asparagus in a single layer and cook for 2 minutes on each side until the asparagus is well seared and slightly wilted.

25 g/1 oz butter

1–2 tablespoons light olive oil

6–8 young asparagus spears, trimmed

rock salt and black pepper

to garnish:

¼ lemon

Parmesan shavings

2 Remove the asparagus from the griddle pan with tongs, and serve on a warmed plate. Pour over the butter and oil mixture and season with the rock salt and black pepper. Garnish with the lemon and Parmesan shavings.

Cooked in a griddle pan or on a barbecue, asparagus has an entirely different taste and texture from boiled or steamed asparagus, particularly if it has been allowed to singe and brown a little, which gives it a rich deep flavour. Choose fine asparagus spears about 1 cm/½ inch in diameter.

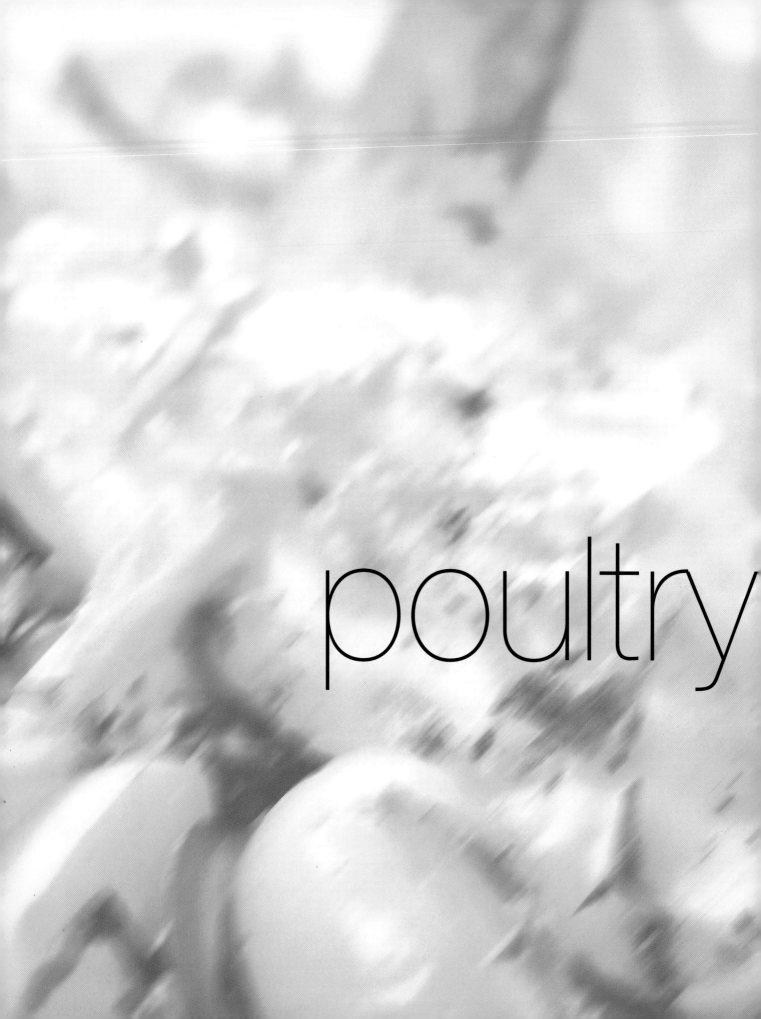

poultry

Griddling brings out the best flavour in many types of poultry and game, such as guinea fowl and turkey, as the quick heat sears the outside and locks the juices and goodness inside.

and game

oriental duck breasts

Serves	**4**
Preparation time	about **20** minutes, plus resting
Cooking time	about **22–26** minutes
Kcal	**230**
KJ	**967**
Protein	**19** g
Fat	**9** g
CHO	**19** g

2 duck breasts, skinned and boned

2 teaspoons vegetable oil

1 large onion, sliced

1 yellow and 2 red peppers, cored,
   deseeded and cut into thin strips

2 teaspoons caster sugar

3 pinches of chilli powder

250 g/8 oz small leaf spinach

sea salt and pepper

bunch of chives, chopped into
   5 cm/2 inch lengths, to garnish

sauce:

1 tablespoon vegetable oil

2 garlic cloves, crushed
   and chopped

juice of 1 lemon

4 tablespoons clear honey

3 tablespoons dark soy sauce

1 Heat the griddle pan and add the duck. Cook for 4–5 minutes on each side for rare, 6–8 minutes if you like it well done. When cooked, place the duck on a carving board to rest.

2 Meanwhile, to make the sauce, heat the oil in a pan, add the garlic and cook until soft, then add the lemon juice, honey and soy sauce. Stir and keep warm.

3 Heat the 2 teaspoons of oil in a wok or large saucepan, add the onion and peppers and stir-fry for 5 minutes. Add the caster sugar, chilli powder and season with salt and pepper to taste. Add the spinach, mix well, and cook for 2 minutes, or until it starts to wilt.

4 Slice the duck very thinly, adding any juices to the sauce. Divide the spinach mixture among 4 warmed plates and arrange the duck on top. Pour the sauce over the duck and garnish with chives.

This is an excellent meal to serve for a dinner party as it is impressive to look at but simple to cook. The duck tastes best rare and pink in the middle and thinly sliced.

szechuan noodles

with chicken and sesame sauce

4	Serves
20 minutes	Preparation time
20–25 minutes	Cooking time
544	Kcal
2280	KJ
25 g	Protein
28 g	Fat
50 g	CHO

2 boneless, skinless chicken
breasts

475 g/15 oz fresh egg noodles or
250 g/8 oz dried noodles

2 tablespoons groundnut oil

sesame sauce:

2 tablespoons groundnut oil

2 garlic cloves, crushed

3 tablespoons tahini paste

1 tablespoon sesame oil

1 tablespoon soy sauce

1–2 teaspoons chilli sauce

1 tablespoon vinegar

125 ml/4 fl oz water

1 teaspoon sugar

sea salt and pepper

to serve:

½ cucumber, sliced into
matchsticks

4–6 spring onions, shredded

250 g/8 oz mooli, peeled and sliced
into matchsticks or 1 bunch
radishes, sliced into matchsticks

125 g/4 oz bean sprouts

Szechuan pepper or Chinese five
spice powder

1 Heat the griddle pan. Season the chicken and griddle for about 8 minutes on each side, or until the juices run clear when pierced with a knife. Place on a chopping board and slice each breast into 6 strips. Put them into a large serving bowl and keep warm.

2 Cook the fresh noodles in boiling water for 1 minute, rinse with cold water and drain well. (If using dried noodles, prepare according to packet instructions.) Heat the groundnut oil in a wok or large frying pan and fry the noodles, stirring constantly, for 2 minutes. Add to the chicken.

3 To make the sesame sauce, add the groundnut oil to the wok or frying pan and fry the garlic until just golden. Remove from the heat and stir in the remaining ingredients and season to taste with salt and pepper.

4 Pour the sauce over the chicken and noodles, sprinkle with cracked Szechuan pepper and serve with the prepared vegetables. Toss the noodles and vegetables together when serving.

Szechuan is a region in western China from which highly fragrant peppercorns hail, as well as a host of unusual, spicy and delicious recipes using them.

spatchcock poussins

with chilli jam

Serves **4**

Preparation time **35** minutes

Cooking time about **35** minutes

Kcal **744**

KJ **3144**

Protein **20** g

Fat **18** g

CHO **135** g

2 poussins

coriander leaves, to garnish

chilli jam:

125 g/4 oz fresh red chillies, cored,
    deseeded and roughly chopped

1 onion, chopped

5 cm/2 inch piece of fresh root
    ginger, peeled and diced

125 ml/4 fl oz white vinegar

500 g/1 lb sugar

1 To make the chilli jam, place the chillies in a blender or food processor with the onion, ginger and vinegar. Process until finely chopped.

2 Place the chilli mixture in a saucepan and add the sugar. Bring to the boil, then simmer for 10 minutes. The mixture should be thick, sticky and jam-like.

3 Prepare the poussins on a board, breast downwards. Cut along the backbone on both sides with poultry shears or a sharp knife and remove. Open out each poussin and place skin-side up on a chopping board. Beat gently with a meat mallet or rolling pin to flatten, but avoid splintering the bones and tearing the skin. Fold the wing tips under the wings, so that they lie flat. Insert 2 skewers through each poussin, criss-cross fashion, to hold them flat.

4 Heat the griddle pan and put on the poussins, flesh-side down. Cook for 15 minutes on each side over a moderate heat until charred and cooked through. To test, insert a sharp knife in the thickest part of the thigh – the juices should run clear. Cut each poussin in half, garnish with the coriander and serve with the chilli jam and French beans, if liked.

Chilli jam can be served as a dip or with charred, crispy griddled meats. It will keep in the refrigerator, covered, for a week. Poussin has a very subtle flavour, and can be bought already spatchcocked.

pigeon breasts
with raspberry peppercorn sauce

4	Serves
10 minutes	Preparation time
20 minutes	Cooking time
530	Kcal
2200	KJ
26 g	Protein
36 g	Fat
8 g	CHO

4 pigeon breasts, skin removed

2 tablespoons extra virgin olive oil

sea salt and pepper

fresh raspberries, to garnish

raspberry peppercorn sauce:

3 teaspoons green peppercorns

3 teaspoons pink peppercorns

75 ml/3 fl oz Cognac

150 ml/¼ pint crème de framboise

150 ml/¼ pint double cream

1 Heat the griddle pan. Slightly flatten the pigeon breasts between two sheets of clingfilm using a rolling pin. When the pan is very hot add the oil and sear the breasts for 1 minute on each side then lower the heat to medium and cook for a further 2 minutes on each side. This should result in pink-coloured breasts. Remove the breasts from the griddle and keep warm in a low oven.

2 To make the raspberry peppercorn sauce, add the peppercorns to the griddle pan, then the Cognac, and carefully set the liquid alight. Keep your face away from the flame and have a lid ready to cover the flaming pan if necessary.

3 When the Cognac has reduced to about 2 tablespoons, add the crème de framboise and reduce by half. Then add the cream and reduce until the sauce has a light coating consistency. Season to taste with salt and pepper. Serve the sauce around or over the pigeon breasts, and garnish with raspberries and extra cracked mixed peppercorns, if liked.

Young pigeons are ideal for this recipe; the searing process seals in their tenderness and the piquant sauce highlights their rich flavour.

devilled chicken
breasts

Serves	**4**
Preparation time	**15** minutes
Cooking time	**25–30** minutes
Kcal	**280**
KJ	**1178**
Protein	**29** g
Fat	**10** g
CHO	**19** g

4 chicken breast fillets

4 raw beetroots, sliced

devil sauce:

2 tablespoons sunflower oil

1 onion, finely chopped

1 garlic clove, crushed

2 tablespoons white wine

4 tablespoons water

2 tablespoons brown sugar

1 tablespoon soy sauce

2 teaspoons Dijon mustard

few drops of Tabasco sauce

2 teaspoons chopped rosemary

2 teaspoons chopped parsley

1 teaspoon chopped thyme

pepper

1 Heat the griddle pan and griddle the chicken for 8 minutes on each side, reducing the heat if necessary. Griddle the beetroot for 4–5 minutes on each side.

2 To make the sauce, heat the oil in a small saucepan, add the onion and garlic and cook for 2–3 minutes until soft. Add the white wine, water, sugar, soy sauce, mustard, Tabasco and pepper to taste. Bring to the boil and simmer until the sauce is reduced by half and thick.

3 Just before serving, add the herbs to the sauce and serve with the griddled chicken and beetroot.

This tangy devil sauce is also good with other griddled meats such as pork.

chicken marinated
with ginger and garlic

4	Serves
20 minutes plus marinating	Preparation time
about **20** minutes	Cooking time
311	Kcal
1307	KJ
29 g	Protein
7 g	Fat
32 g	CHO

1 Place the chicken in a glass dish. Add the ginger, garlic and chilli, mix well and leave to marinate in the refrigerator for at least 2 hours. (If time is short, marinate them for 1 hour and do not put them in the refrigerator.)

4 small chicken breast fillets, cut into thin strips

5 cm/2 inch piece of fresh root ginger, peeled and finely diced

4 large garlic cloves, crushed

1 green chilli, deseeded and finely chopped

1 bunch of spring onions, cut into 5 cm/2 inch lengths

150 g/5 oz rice noodles

1 tablespoon sesame oil

2 tablespoons soy sauce

1 bunch of coriander, chopped

grated rind and juice of 1 lime

sea salt and pepper

2 Cut the spring onion lengths into very thin strips. Place them in cold water, where they will curl.

3 Heat the griddle pan. Put the chicken on the griddle and cook for 7 minutes on each side.

4 Meanwhile, bring a saucepan of lightly salted water to the boil, add the rice noodles and cook for 2 minutes. Drain well, then add the sesame oil, soy sauce, coriander, lime rind and juice, and season to taste with salt and pepper, then toss well.

5 Add the drained spring onions to the chicken and cook, stirring, for 30 seconds. Arrange on a bed of noodles and serve at once.

Place ice cubes in the water to make it as cold as possible. The spring onion strips will become even more curly the longer they are left in the cold water.

stuffed guinea fowl

Serves	**4**
Preparation time	**15** minutes
Cooking time	**16–20** minutes
Kcal	**410**
KJ	**1700**
Protein	**30** g
Fat	**31** g
CHO	**2** g

125 g/4 oz ricotta cheese

75 g/3 oz sun-dried tomatoes, chopped

4 spring onions, chopped

4 guinea fowl breasts

sea salt and pepper

1 In a large bowl, mix together the ricotta cheese with the chopped tomatoes, spring onions and season to taste with salt and pepper. Heat the griddle pan.

2 To prepare each guinea fowl breast for stuffing, use a sharp knife and with the underneath of the breast facing you, carefully run the knife along the length of the breast and then inwards, making a long flat pocket.

3 Divide the stuffing among the 4 breasts and stuff the ricotta mixture in carefully.

4 Place the breasts on the griddle pan and cook for 8–10 minutes on each side, depending on the size of the breasts. To test, pierce the meat with a small sharp knife at the thickest part – the juices should run clear when fully cooked. Serve either hot or at room temperature.

Guinea fowl was originally a game bird, its flesh and flavour are similar to chicken and pheasant. It is tender but has a mild flavour.

griddled and
roast guinea fowl joints

4	Serves
10 minutes	Preparation time
about **40** minutes	Cooking time
467	Kcal
1938	KJ
35 g	Protein
36 g	Fat
1 g	CHO

1 Heat the griddle pan, put on the guinea fowl joints and cook for about 6 minutes on each side. The skin should be quite charred, which will give the guinea fowl a good flavour.

1 x 1.75 kg/3½ lb guinea fowl, jointed into 8 pieces
2 tablespoons Dijon mustard
grated rind and juice of 2 lemons, plus extra pared rind, to garnish
vegetable oil
sea salt flakes and pepper
coriander leaves, to garnish
sweet potato slices, griddled, to serve (optional)

2 Mix the mustard, lemon rind and juice in a bowl and season to taste with salt and pepper.

3 Remove the guinea fowl from the pan and place in a lightly oiled roasting tin. Using a pastry brush, brush the joints with the mustard mixture, then place on the top shelf of a preheated oven, 200°C (400°F), Gas Mark 6, for 20 minutes. To test, insert a sharp knife into the thickest part of each joint – the juices should run clear.

4 Transfer the guinea fowl to warmed serving plates. Garnish with the lemon rind and coriander and serve with griddled sweet potatoes, if liked.

Mustard pastes on poultry are easy to make and tasty. Griddling helps to form a lovely crust, while finishing it off in the oven ensures that it is thoroughly cooked.

pheasant breasts
with spinach salad

Serves	**4**
Preparation time	**15** minutes, plus resting
Cooking time	about **10** minutes
Kcal	**626**
KJ	**2599**
Protein	**47** g
Fat	**43** g
CHO	**14** g

1 Heat the griddle pan. Place the pheasant breasts on the griddle and cook for about 3–4 minutes on each side.

2 Place the spinach, avocado, red pepper, olives and artichoke hearts in a bowl. Season to taste with salt and pepper and mix well.

8 pheasant breasts

500 g/1 lb trimmed baby spinach leaves

2 avocados, peeled and chopped

1 red pepper, roasted and chopped

75 g/3 oz olives, pitted

200 g/7 oz artichoke hearts

dressing:

1 garlic clove, crushed and chopped

75 ml/3 fl oz olive oil

2 tablespoons wine vinegar

1 tablespoon wholegrain mustard

1 teaspoon sugar

sea salt and pepper

3 To make the dressing, place the garlic, olive oil, vinegar, mustard and sugar in a small bowl and mix well until smooth. Season to taste with salt and pepper and adjust the consistency, if necessary, with a little more oil or vinegar. Pour the dressing over the salad and toss.

4 Remove the pheasant breasts from the griddle when cooked and allow to rest for 5 minutes. Slice either thickly or thinly, as you prefer, add to the salad and toss well. Serve with crusty country bread or small jacket potatoes.

It may seem rather lavish to eat just the pheasant breasts, but use the carcasses to make a good game stock, for an old-fashioned barley and vegetable soup with bacon. Ask the butcher to remove the breasts from the pheasants.

lemon chicken salad

4	Serves
25 minutes	Preparation time
about **20** minutes	Cooking time
849	Kcal
3524	KJ
32 g	Protein
69 g	Fat
27 g	CHO

1 juicy lemon

2 egg yolks

2 teaspoons Dijon mustard

1 teaspoon white wine vinegar

250 ml/8 fl oz olive oil

4 chicken breast fillets

1 Cos lettuce, leaves torn

500 g/1 lb new potatoes, cooked
   and still warm

125 g/4 oz cherry tomatoes, halved

bunch of flat leaf parsley, roughly
   chopped

1 red onion, sliced

sea salt and pepper

1 Remove the rind from the lemon with a sharp knife or lemon zester, then peel off all the skin. Divide the lemon into segments and squeeze out all the juice, removing any pips. Place the lemon rind, flesh and juice, the egg yolks, mustard, vinegar and salt and pepper in a food processor and blend until smooth, or use a hand-held blender. With the machine still running, drizzle in the oil until the sauce starts to thicken. Continue until all the oil has been added.

2 Heat the griddle pan. Put on the chicken and cook for about 8 minutes on each side, reducing the heat if it is charring too much.

3 Arrange the lettuce in a large bowl. Chop the potatoes and place in the bowl. Add the tomatoes, sprinkle with chopped parsley and sliced onion; season to taste with salt and pepper.

4 Arrange the chicken on top of the salad, pour the sauce over and serve.

This is a lovely quick supper dish, and the combination of warm chicken on a crunchy salad is delicious with the mustardy dressing.

tandoori turkey
with ginger dressing

Serves	**4**
Preparation time	**20** minutes, plus standing
Cooking time	**10–12** minutes
Kcal	**240**
KJ	**1018**
Protein	**45** g
Fat	**3** g
CHO	**9** g

**4 x 175 g/6 oz thin escalopes of
   turkey**

ginger dressing:

300 ml/½ pint natural yogurt
**2.5 cm/1 inch piece of fresh root
   ginger, peeled and finely chopped**
**1 garlic clove, crushed and
   chopped**
2 teaspoons paprika
1 teaspoon chilli powder
**4 tomatoes, skinned, deseeded
   and chopped**
2 tablespoons chopped coriander
grated rind and juice of ½ lemon
sea salt and pepper

to garnish:

**2 limes, cut into wedges and
   griddled, plus shavings of rind**
parsley sprigs

1 To make the dressing, mix together all the ingredients in a bowl and season to taste with salt and pepper.

2 Heat the griddle pan, put on the turkey and cook for 4–5 minutes on each side. Remove the turkey from the griddle and slice it into long strips. Place the strips in the bowl with the dressing. Mix well, then allow to stand for 30 minutes to absorb the flavours.

3 Garnish with the lime, a few shavings of lime rind and parsley.

An unusual recipe, this is particularly refreshing for those long summer days in the garden. Serve with warm naan bread and a green salad, if liked.

chicken legs
in sticky barbecue sauce

4	Serves
10 minutes, plus marinating	Preparation time
30–40 minutes	Cooking time
440	Kcal
1840	KJ
23 g	Protein
27 g	Fat
28 g	CHO

1 To make the barbecue sauce, heat the olive oil in a saucepan, add the onion and fry until it is just starting to colour, then add the remaining sauce ingredients and combine well. Simmer gently, uncovered, for 10 minutes.

8 chicken legs, with skin on

sea salt and cayenne pepper

barbecue sauce:

2 tablespoons olive oil

1 large onion, grated

1 tablespoon tomato purée

4 tablespoons mushroom ketchup

2 tablespoons red wine vinegar

2 tablespoons demerara sugar

2 tablespoons clear honey

2 teaspoons English mustard

2 tablespoons Worcestershire sauce

150 ml/¼ pint water

2 Place the chicken legs in a shallow container, season lightly with salt and pepper then pour over the sauce. Cover and set aside to marinate for a minimum of 30 minutes or longer if possible.

3 Heat the griddle pan. Put on the chicken for 10–15 minutes over a low heat, turning half way through cooking. Brush with any remaining barbecue sauce and serve hot or at room temperature.

The combination of ingredients in this marinade give the chicken a wonderful flavour and crunchy coating. Serve with a crisp green salad.

celebration chicken

with warm lemon hollandaise

Serves **4**

Preparation time: **25** minutes

Cooking time: about **50** minutes

Kcal **964**

KJ **3960**

Protein **42** g

Fat **76** g

CHO **28** g

1 x 1.75 kg/3½ lb chicken, boned

1 curly endive lettuce

375 g/12 oz new potatoes, cooked
and sliced

8 plum tomatoes, skinned and
chopped

1 onion, griddled and sliced

175 g/6 oz asparagus, griddled

125 g/4 oz green beans, cooked

1 bunch of radishes, sliced

1 bunch of flat leaf parsley,
chopped

lemon hollandaise:

175 g/6 oz unsalted butter

2 large egg yolks

1 teaspoon Dijon mustard

juice of 1 lemon

sea salt and pepper

1 Heat the griddle pan, put on the chicken, skin-side down, and cook for 20 minutes on each side. The outside of the chicken should be beautifully charred when cooked. To test that it is cooked, insert a sharp knife into the thickest part of the thigh – the juices should run clear.

2 Meanwhile, line a large serving platter with lettuce leaves, then arrange the potatoes, tomatoes, onion, asparagus, beans and radishes on top.

3 To make the hollandaise, melt the butter slowly in a small saucepan. Using a food processor or hand-held blender, process the egg yolks, mustard and lemon juice until smooth. With the machine still running, slowly pour in the butter. Season with salt and pepper, then pour the sauce into a small bowl and place it in a *bain-marie*, or a saucepan of warm water, so that it keeps warm.

4 Remove the chicken from the heat, place on a carving board and slice thinly. Arrange the chicken over the salad and season. Sprinkle with the chopped parsley and spoon over the hollandaise sauce.

A *bain-marie* is a large shallow pan in which saucepans, bowls or dishes can be placed in simmering water. It is ideal when making sauces or egg custards as it prevents them from curdling.

chicken satay
with peanut and chilli sauce

4	Serves
35 minutes, plus marinating	Preparation time
about **15** minutes	Cooking time
388	Kcal
1633	KJ
27 g	Protein
19 g	Fat
28 g	CHO

475 g/15 oz boneless, skinless

chicken breasts

marinade:

2 teaspoons coriander seeds

½ teaspoon cumin seeds

2 garlic cloves, coarsely chopped

½ teaspoon coarsely chopped

   ginger

1 teaspoon fresh or ground

   turmeric, coarsely chopped

4 red shallots, coarsely chopped

1 teaspoon sea salt

2 tablespoons sugar

2 tablespoons groundnut oil

peanut and chilli sauce:

2 chillies, chopped

2 garlic cloves, chopped

1 stalk of lemon grass, chopped

1 teaspoon fresh or ground

   turmeric, chopped

2 tablespoons oil

450 ml/¾ pint coconut milk

1 tablespoon tamarind water (made

   by soaking tamarind paste in hot

   water)

2 tablespoons sugar

½ teaspoon salt

4 tablespoons chopped peanuts

1 Slice the chicken breasts into 10 cm x 1 cm/4 inch x ½ inch strips and place in a large bowl. In a food processor, or using a pestle and mortar, process all the marinade ingredients to a smooth paste. Add the marinade to the chicken, mix well and set aside to marinate for at least 1 hour.

2 To make the sauce, process the chillies, garlic, lemon grass and turmeric in a food processor or with a pestle and mortar to make a paste. Heat the oil in a wok or deep frying pan and stir in the paste. Add the coconut milk and bring to the boil. Add the remaining sauce ingredients and simmer for 3 minutes. Pour into a serving bowl and set aside.

3 Heat the griddle pan. Thread the chicken on to 20 pre-soaked wooden satay sticks, place the sticks on the hot griddle and cook for 2 minutes on each side or until cooked through. Serve with the peanut and chilli sauce and with boiled white rice, if liked.

Use lemon or lime juice as alternatives to tamarind water.

balsamic chicken
with rosemary

Serves	**4**
Preparation time	**15** minutes
Cooking time	**25–30** minutes
Kcal	**446**
KJ	**1849**
Protein	**27** g
Fat	**35** g
CHO	**69** g

8 boneless chicken thighs

8 rosemary sprigs

4 garlic cloves, sliced lengthways

2 red onions, cut into wedges

3 tablespoons olive oil

1½ tablespoons balsamic vinegar

sea salt and pepper

1 Trim any excess fat off the chicken thighs and lay out flat.

2 Using a satay stick, weave holes through the chicken, following closely with the rosemary sprig, and weave until all the sprig is woven into the chicken.

3 Push the slivers of garlic into the holes through which the rosemary is woven.

4 Heat the griddle pan. Place the chicken on the griddle and cook for 8–10 minutes on each side, or until the juices run clear when the chicken is pierced with a knife.

5 Add the onions to the chicken and cook for 8 minutes. Arrange the chicken and onions on a serving dish and drizzle over the olive oil and balsamic vinegar. Season to taste with salt and pepper and serve with green vegetables or with pasta.

Balsamic vinegar is made in and around Modena in northern Italy. Its dark and mellow colour makes a great decorative touch when drizzled with a little olive oil around the edge of a plate.

pheasant
with juniper cream sauce

4	Serves
20 minutes, plus resting	Preparation time
about **40** minutes	Cooking time
470	Kcal
1950	KJ
36 g	Protein
33 g	Fat
3 g	CHO

1 Heat the olive oil and butter in the griddle pan, add the pheasant and cook for about 4–5 minutes until brown all over. Transfer the pheasant to a roasting tin and roast it on its side in a preheated oven, 220°C (425°F), Gas Mark 7, for 25 minutes, turning the bird over half way through the cooking time. Remove the pheasant from the pan and set aside to rest for about 10 minutes before carving.

1 tablespoon extra virgin olive oil

25 g/1 oz butter

1 large pheasant

fresh blueberries, to garnish

juniper cream sauce:

25 g/1 oz unsalted butter

4 shallots, finely chopped

6 tablespoons white wine

1 heaped teaspoon chopped juniper berries

125 ml/4 fl oz game or chicken stock

4 tablespoons double cream

sea salt and pepper

2 Meanwhile, make the sauce in the griddle pan. Heat the griddle pan, add the butter and sauté the shallots until soft. Add the white wine and the juniper berries and cook until reduced by half. Pour in the stock and reduce by half and then stir in the cream. Deglaze the roasting tin with a little water and add the juices to the cream sauce. Season the sauce with salt and pepper to taste, then strain it and serve with the pheasant. Garnish with the fresh blueberries.

If you have a cast-iron griddle pan with a cast-iron handle the whole pan can be placed in the oven instead of transferring the pheasant to a roasting tin. Make the sauce separately.

chicken and fennel
with dill dressing

Serves	**4**
Preparation time	**10** minutes
Cooking time	about **30** minutes
Kcal	**329**
KJ	**1369**
Protein	**34** g
Fat	**21** g
CHO	**1** g

8 chicken thighs, boned

2 fennel bulbs, sliced

4 tablespoons olive oil

1 tablespoon balsamic vinegar

bunch of dill, chopped

sea salt and pepper

1 Heat the griddle pan, put on the chicken and cook for 6–8 minutes on each side. Remove from the pan and keep warm.

2 Add the fennel to the pan and cook for 4 minutes on each side. Remove from the pan, set aside and keep warm. Return the chicken to the pan and cook for another 3 minutes on each side to give a good crust to the skin.

3 In a small bowl, mix together the oil, vinegar, and dill and season with salt and pepper to taste. To serve, layer the chicken and fennel and pour the dressing over.

This is a fabulous-looking dish, but really quite simple to prepare. It can be served either hot or at room temperature.

duck breasts
with pomegranate and walnuts

4	Serves
25 minutes	Preparation time
20–25 minutes	Cooking time
484	Kcal
2009	KJ
32 g	Protein
33 g	Fat
9 g	CHO

1 Remove a few tablespoons of the pomegranate seeds and set aside. Squeeze the rest of the halves in a citrus juicer and strain the juice.

3 ripe pomegranates, cut in half

4 duck breasts (preferably wild duck)

2 tablespoons olive oil

150 ml/¼ pint red wine

pinch of thyme

12 fresh (wet) walnuts, cracked open and peeled, or dried walnuts, peeled (see below)

1 tablespoon arrowroot

2 tablespoons cold water

sea salt and pepper

2 Heat the griddle pan. Meanwhile, using a rolling pin, slightly flatten the duck breasts between 2 sheets of clingfilm. Heat the olive oil in the griddle pan and cook the duck skin-side down for 8 minutes. Turn over and cook for a further 5 minutes.

3 Put the cooked breasts on warmed plates and drain the excess oil out of the griddle pan. Deglaze the pan with the wine and add the thyme, pomegranate juice and the walnuts. Simmer gently, as walnuts burn very quickly, for 2 minutes and then season with salt and pepper to taste.

4 Combine the arrowroot with the cold water, add to the sauce and simmer gently for 1 minute. Add the reserved pomegranate seeds and pour over the duck. Serve immediately.

If fresh walnuts are not available use dried walnuts and dip them in boiling water for 30 seconds to loosen the inner skin before peeling. The sharpness of the inner skin can make them taste slightly bitter.

meat

Griddling is a fantastic way of cooking meat such as lamb, beef, pork and rabbit as it sears in all the flavour and keeps the meat tender.

dishes

mediterranean lamb
cakes with salsa verde

Serves	**4**
Preparation time	**25** minutes
Cooking time	**15–20** minutes
Kcal	**420**
KJ	**1747**
Protein	**29** g
Fat	**33** g
CHO	**2** g

500 g/1 lb lean minced lamb

2 garlic cloves, crushed and chopped

1 tablespoon grated Parmesan cheese

1 tablespoon pitted and chopped olives

1 tablespoon chopped basil

finely grated rind of 1 lemon

1 tablespoon chopped, roasted pine nuts

1 egg white

mixed salad leaves, to serve

1 Place the minced lamb, garlic, Parmesan, olives, basil, lemon rind, pine nuts and egg white in a bowl and mix well with a fork. Shape with damp hands into 8 even-sized patties.

2 Mix together all the salsa ingredients in a bowl. For a smooth textured salsa, process the ingredients in a blender or food processor. Taste and adjust the seasoning if necessary.

salsa verde:

3 tablespoons chopped parsley

2 tablespoons chopped mint

1 tablespoon chopped chives

4 tablespoons olive oil

1 tablespoon chopped capers

3 garlic cloves, crushed and chopped

juice of 1 lemon

1 small onion, chopped

1 ripe avocado, pitted and chopped

few drops of Tabasco sauce

sea salt and pepper

3 Heat the griddle pan and put on the lamb cakes. Cook on each side for 6–8 minutes, until charred and firm. Serve in stacks with the mixed salad leaves and the salsa.

Serve this delicious dish accompanied by steamed new potatoes and mangetout or sugar snap peas.

moroccan lamb

keftas

4	Serves
30 minutes, plus standiing	Preparation time
8–10 minutes	Cooking time
230	Kcal
967	KJ
27 g	Protein
12 g	Fat
4 g	CHO

475 g/15 oz minced lamb or beef

marinade:

1 teaspoon freshly ground cumin

2 teaspoons paprika

1 teaspoon hot chilli powder

1 teaspoon cinnamon

pinch of saffron, soaked in

  1 teaspoon of hot water

1 bunch of parsley, chopped

1 bunch of mint, chopped

1 onion, finely chopped

2 garlic cloves, finely chopped

½ preserved lemon, finely chopped

1 egg, beaten

sea salt

1 Mix together all the ingredients for the marinade and set aside for up to 1 hour to allow the flavours to blend. Then take pieces of mince, about the size of an egg, and with wet hands wrap the pieces around 16 metal or wooden skewers, shaping them into a sausage shape about 6–8 cm/2½–3½ inches long.

2 Heat the griddle pan. Griddle the keftas, turning constantly, for 8–10 minutes or until cooked through. Serve with couscous and glasses of mint tea, if liked.

If using wooden skewers, be sure to soak them in cold water before use. If possible, make the keftas a day in advance to allow the flavours to develop. Preserved lemons can be bought from most delicatessens.

loin of lamb
with blue cheese polenta

Serves	**6**
Preparation time:	**15** minutes
Cooking time:	about **45** minutes
Kcal	**630**
KJ	**2622**
Protein	**49** g
Fat	**39** g
CHO	**21** g

1 Heat the griddle pan. Add the lamb loins and sear them all over for 10–12 minutes. Transfer to a lightly oiled roasting tin and cook in a preheated oven, 200°C (400°F), Gas Mark 6, for about 10–15 minutes for rare, or for 20–25 minutes for well done.

2 Bring the water to the boil in a pan, add the polenta and mix well. Simmer, stirring, for 10 minutes until the polenta thickens and the water is absorbed. Add the butter, dolcelatte and mascarpone torta, marjoram and season to taste. Mix well and keep warm.

2 loins of lamb, about
    1.25 kg/2½ lb, boned and rolled
vegetable oil
1 litre/1¾ pints water
175 g/6 oz polenta
75 g/3 oz butter
175 g/6 oz dolcelatte and
    mascarpone torta
3 tablespoons chopped marjoram
sea salt and pepper

3 Allow the lamb to rest for about 5 minutes. Serve sliced, with the blue cheese polenta.

Polenta is a yellow maize flour from northern Italy. It is rich in vitamins. Use instant or quick cooking polenta and stir continuously or it will become lumpy.

herb lamb chops
with balsamic vinegar

4	Serves
10 minutes, plus marinating	Preparation time
10–15 minutes	Cooking time
373	Kcal
1548	KJ
25 g	Protein
31 g	Fat
0 g	CHO

4 double lamb chump chops

1 bunch of mint, chopped

1 rosemary sprig, chopped

3 tablespoons balsamic vinegar

sea salt and pepper

1 Place the lamb chops on a large flat dish. Sprinkle with the mint and rosemary and season the chops with salt and pepper to taste. Spoon over the balsamic vinegar, cover and leave to marinate overnight or for as long as possible. If time is short, then 30 minutes out of the refrigerator is sufficient.

2 Heat the griddle pan. Place the chops on the griddle and cook for 4–6 minutes on each side.

3 Heat up any excess marinade juices in the griddle pan and pour over the chops. Serve with mustard mashed potatoes (see below) and fried onions, if liked.

To make mustard mashed potatoes: cut 750 g/1½ lb potatoes into large chunks and boil for about 20 minutes, until tender. Drain well, return to the pan and add 50 g/2 oz butter, 1 tablespoon wholegrain mustard and 150 ml/¼ pint single cream; mash well. Season to taste.

hamburgers
with griddled radicchio

Serves	**4**
Preparation time	**30** minutes
Cooking time	**15** minutes
Kcal	**1267**
KJ	**5278**
Protein	**52** g
Fat	**91** g
CHO	**63** g

750 g/1½ lb lean beef, finely minced

1 small onion, finely chopped

2 tablespoons Worcestershire sauce

4 brown bread baps, or ciabatta rolls

1 large head radicchio, cut into

  6 wedges

2 beef tomatoes, skinned and sliced

sea salt and pepper

Sweet Potato Chips, to serve

  (see page 15)

mustard mayonnaise:

2 egg yolks

1 tablespoon white wine vinegar

1 tablespoon Dijon mustard

1 tablespoon coarse grain mustard

300 ml/½ pint grapeseed oil

1 Place the meat, onion, Worcestershire sauce and seasoning in a bowl and mix with a fork. With wet hands, shape the meat into 4 hamburgers to fit into the baps or rolls.

2 To make the mustard mayonnaise, place the egg yolks, vinegar and Dijon and coarse grain mustards in a bowl and mix with a hand-held blender or use a food processor. Slowly pour in the oil, continuing to blend, until the mixture is smooth and creamy. Season with salt and pepper.

3 Heat the griddle pan, put on the prepared burgers and cook for 3 minutes on each side for rare, or 5 minutes for well done. Remove from the griddle and keep warm. Cut the baps in half and place cut-side down on the griddle to toast and absorb any meat juices. Cook the radicchio wedges for 1 minute on each side.

4 To assemble, spread the bottom half of each bap with mustard mayonnaise, then add a wedge of radicchio, a burger, more mustard mayonnaise, half a slice of tomato, another radicchio wedge and more mustard mayonnaise. Cover with the top half of the bap and serve immediately with griddled sweet potato chips.

Home-made hamburgers are the best: you can choose the cut of meat and season according to taste. Try adding herbs, Tabasco sauce or chopped nuts.

summer vegetable
and sausage pie

8	Serves
35 minutes	Preparation time
1¼–1½ hours	Cooking time
557	Kcal
2326	KJ
18 g	Protein
35 g	Fat
46 g	CHO

1 red pepper, cored, deseeded and
  quartered

1 yellow pepper, cored, deseeded
  and quartered

500 g/1 lb Cumberland or
  Lincolnshire sausages, skinned

1 bunch basil leaves, roughly
  chopped

1 aubergine, sliced

1 bunch of spring onions, sliced

250 g/8 oz haloumi cheese, sliced

375 g/12 oz courgettes, sliced
  lengthways

pastry:

375 g/12 oz plain flour

175 ml/6 fl oz water

75 g/3 oz butter

beaten egg, to glaze

salt and pepper

1 Heat the griddle pan, then griddle the peppers skin-side up, until the skin is charred and slightly blackened all over.

2 To make the pastry, season the flour in a mixing bowl. Pour the water into a pan, add the butter and bring to a simmer. Make a well in the centre of the flour, pour in the hot liquid and mix with a fork to form a firm dough. Knead briefly, then wrap in clingfilm and set aside to rest for 15 minutes.

3 Roll out about two-thirds of the dough on a lightly floured flat surface and carefully line a greased 20 cm/8 inch springform tin, pinching together any cracks that appear in the pastry. Press the sausagemeat firmly into the base of the pastry case, then carefully layer the peppers, basil, aubergine, spring onions, haloumi and courgettes, seasoning with salt and pepper between each of the layers.

4 Brush the edge of the pastry with a little beaten egg, then roll out the remaining pastry and cover the pie. Press the edges to seal, then pinch the edges all round to decorate. Make a hole in the centre of the pie to allow the steam to escape during the cooking time, then brush the top with egg to glaze the pie.

5 Bake in a preheated oven, 190°C (375°F), Gas Mark 5, for 1–1¼ hours until the pastry is golden brown. Cool in the tin for 15 minutes. Serve the pie warm or cold, cut into slices.

liver and bacon
with roasted tomato chutney

Serves **4**

Preparation time **10** minutes

Cooking time about **55** minutes

Kcal **569**

KJ **2380**

Protein **37** g

Fat **33** g

CHO **33** g

1 Spoon 2 tablespoons of the olive oil into a roasting tin and heat in a preheated oven, 220°C (425°F), Gas Mark 7. Add the tomatoes, turn them in the oil to coat well, and place the tin at the top of the oven. Roast the tomatoes for 40 minutes, or until they begin to darken slightly around the edges.

3 tablespoons olive oil

750 g/1½ lb tomatoes, halved and
   green cores removed

1 red onion, sliced

1 garlic clove, crushed and
   chopped

50 g/2 oz raisins

50 g/2 oz brown sugar

3 tablespoons white wine vinegar

1 teaspoon chopped rosemary

1 teaspoon black mustard seeds

8 rashers of rindless smoked
   streaky bacon

4 slices of calves' liver, about
   125 g/4 oz each

sea salt and pepper

rosemary sprigs, to garnish

2 Heat the remaining tablespoon of olive oil in a frying pan and add the onion and garlic. Fry over a low heat for 5 minutes, then add the raisins, brown sugar, vinegar, rosemary, mustard seeds and season to taste with salt and pepper. Mix well and simmer for 2 minutes. Mix in the tomatoes, then remove from the heat.

3 Heat the griddle pan, put on the bacon and cook until crispy, about 2 minutes on each side. Keep warm. Place the calves' liver on the griddle and cook for 2 minutes on each side for pink, or cook 4 minutes for well done. Serve at once with the bacon and roasted tomato chutney, garnished with rosemary sprigs.

This tomato chutney makes the simple dish of liver and bacon into a visual and tasty delight. Make more chutney if you wish and store it in the refrigerator to serve with cold meats.

spanish chorizo
and fig brochettes

4	Serves
15 minutes	Preparation time
6–8 minutes	Cooking time
367	Kcal
1532	KJ
18 g	Protein
25 g	Fat
16 g	CHO

4 chorizo sausages

8 fresh figs

marinade:

1 tablespoons olive oil

2 garlic cloves, crushed

4 tablespoons red wine

1 tablespoon clear honey

1 bay leaf

1 tablespoon chopped parsley

sea salt and pepper

1 Thread the chorizo and figs alternately on to 8 metal or wooden skewers. If using wooden skewers, soak them in cold water before use.

2 To make the marinade, heat the oil in a frying pan and gently fry the garlic until golden. Add the wine, stir, then add the honey, bay leaf and parsley and season to taste with salt and pepper. Cook for 2 minutes.

3 Heat the griddle pan. Place the skewers on the griddle and brush generously with the marinade. Cook for 2–3 minutes on each side or until the sausages are slightly blackened and crispy.

Chorizo is a coarse-textured, dried, spicy Spanish sausage, flavoured with garlic and chilli.

veal escalopes
with wilted spinach salad

Serves	**4**
Preparation time	**15–20** minutes
Cooking time	**10–15** minutes
Kcal	**440**
KJ	**1840**
Protein	**52** g
Fat	**25** g
CHO	**2** g

150 g/5 oz Parmesan cheese, coarsely grated

4 tablespoons chopped flat leaf parsley

2 eggs

4 x 150 g/5 oz veal escalopes

2 lemons, halved

sea salt and pepper

1 Mix together the Parmesan and parsley on a flat plate and season with salt and pepper. Beat the eggs in a large, shallow dish. Dip the escalopes into the beaten egg and then into the Parmesan mixture, pressing the mixture on to the escalopes to coat well. Heat the griddle pan, put on the escalopes and cook on each side for 2 minutes. Remove and keep warm. Add the lemons to the griddle, cut-side down, and cook for 1–2 minutes, until charred.

wilted spinach salad:

250 g/8 oz spinach, roughly torn

125 g/4 oz cherry tomatoes, halved

2 tablespoons olive oil

1 tablespoon balsamic vinegar

2 To make the salad, place the spinach and tomatoes in a wok or large saucepan and toss and cook for 1–2 minutes, to warm and slightly wilt the spinach. Add the oil and vinegar, season and toss well.

3 Serve the veal over the spinach salad, with charred lemon halves.

The Parmesan cheese turns into a golden, crunchy crust on the meat. The warm and wilted spinach salad makes a tasty and colourful accompaniment.

pork fillet
with herbs and pistachios

4		Serves
20	minutes	Preparation time
15–20	minutes	Cooking time
404		Kcal
1688		KJ
42	g	Protein
30	g	Fat
9	g	CHO

1 Heat the oil in a small saucepan, add the shallots and garlic and cook for 3 minutes, but do not allow to brown. Sprinkle in the flour and stir. Stir in the wine, cook gently until the sauce is smooth and season to taste with salt and pepper.

1 tablespoon soya or sunflower oil

4 shallots or small onions, finely chopped

1 garlic clove, crushed and chopped

1 tablespoon wholemeal flour

150 ml/¼ pint dry white wine

750 g/1½ lb pork fillet, thinly sliced

125 g/4 oz broccoli florets

2 tablespoons chopped sage leaves

2 tablespoons chopped chives

2 tablespoons chopped thyme

50 g/2 oz pistachio nuts, shelled and chopped

1 orange pepper, deseeded and quartered (optional)

sea salt and pepper

2 Heat the griddle pan and add the sliced pork fillet, in batches. Cook each batch for 3 minutes on each side and keep warm. Meanwhile, blanch the broccoli in a small saucepan of boiling water for 1 minute, drain, then add to the sauce.

3 Add the herbs and pistachio nuts and orange pepper, if using, to the sauce and heat through, stirring, for 1 minute. Serve the pork tossed with the sauce.

Pistachio nuts have a pale green flesh and purple skins. They originated in the Middle East and Central Asia. The beige coloured shells split when the kernels are ripe.

green peppercorn
steaks

Serves	**4**
Preparation time	**5** minutes
Cooking time	**6–8** minutes
Kcal	**114**
KJ	**479**
Protein	**17** g
Fat	**4** g
CHO	**4** g

4 lean fillet steaks, each about

   75 g/3 oz

1 tablespoon green peppercorns in

   brine, drained

2 tablespoons light soy sauce

1 teaspoon balsamic vinegar

8 cherry tomatoes, halved

thyme sprigs, to garnish

1 Heat the griddle pan until it is very hot. Cook the steaks for about 2–3 minutes on each side. Remove from the griddle and keep hot.

2 Add the peppercorns, soy sauce, balsamic vinegar and cherry tomatoes to the griddle pan. Allow the liquids to sizzle for 2 minutes, or until the tomatoes are soft. Serve the sauce spooned over the steaks and garnish with the thyme sprigs.

Serve this hearty yet low-fat meal with boiled potatoes or mustard mashed potatoes (see page 61).

venison steaks
with red fruit sauce

4	Serves
10 minutes, plus marinating	Preparation time
about **20** minutes	Cooking time
270	Kcal
1153	KJ
39 g	Protein
3 g	Fat
23 g	CHO

1 Mix the juniper berries with salt and pepper and spread over both sides of the venison steaks. Set aside to allow the flavours to absorb, for at least 1 hour but preferably overnight.

1 teaspoon crushed juniper berries

4 x 175 g/6 oz venison steaks, from the fillet or loin

sea salt and pepper

shredded orange rind, to garnish

2 To make the sauce, place the ingredients in a small saucepan and simmer gently for 10 minutes, stirring constantly.

red fruit sauce:

125 g/4 oz redcurrant jelly

125 g/4 oz cranberries

grated rind and juice of 1 orange

2 tablespoons red wine

3 Heat the griddle pan. Put on the venison steaks and cook for 3 minutes on each side for rare, or 5 minutes for well done. Serve immediately with the red fruit sauce poured over the top and garnished with the shredded orange rind.

Venison steak from the loin or fillet is not always available, so ask your butcher if you can use another cut. This makes a lovely winter dinner, rich in colour and flavour.

roast beef
and tomatoes with mustard sauce

Serves	**8**
Preparation time	**20** minutes
Cooking time	**50** minutes
Kcal	**262**
KJ	**1104**
Protein	**34** g
Fat	**10** g
CHO	**11** g

1.25 kg/2½ lb fillet of beef

1 tablespoon olive oil, plus extra
   for oiling

1 garlic clove, sliced

2 red onions, sliced

16 small tomatoes

2 tablespoons Dijon mustard

2 tablespoons coarse grain
   mustard

2 tablespoons clear honey

2 tablespoons chopped coriander

sea salt and pepper

1 Heat the griddle pan. Season the beef fillet with salt and pepper and pat in the seasoning. Place the fillet on the griddle and cook for about 20–25 minutes, turning regularly, until the fillet is charred on all sides.

2 Transfer the fillet to a lightly oiled roasting tin and cook in a preheated oven, 220°C (425°F), Gas Mark 7, for 10–15 minutes for rare or 20–25 minutes for medium. Remove from the oven and allow to rest for 10 minutes.

3 Heat the oil in a pan. Add the garlic and onions and cook for 5 minutes. Add the tomatoes, season to taste and warm through for 3 minutes.

4 Warm the two mustards in a small saucepan with the honey. Stir until blended. Add the coriander to the tomato mixture. Slice the fillet and serve on a bed of the tomato mixture, with the mustard sauce drizzled over.

This is a somewhat lavish but totally delicious meal, perfect for serving at a dinner party or a special occasion.

rabbit
with balsamic vinaigrette

(as a starter) **6**	Serves
15 minutes, plus marinating	Preparation time
5–7 minutes	Cooking time
730	Kcal
3035	KJ
21 g	Protein
56 g	Fat
32 g	CHO

4 rabbit loins, boned

250 g/8 oz green beans, trimmed

125 g/4 oz mixed salad leaves

croûtons:

1 French stick, cut into

  2.5 cm/1 inch diagonal slices

125 g/4 oz unsalted butter,

  softened

2 tablespoons wholegrain mustard

marinade:

2 shallots, finely sliced

2 garlic cloves, crushed

200 ml/7 fl oz olive oil

200 ml/7 fl oz dry white wine

1 bunch of tarragon, chopped

1 bunch flat leaf parsley, chopped

freshly cracked pepper

balsamic vinaigrette:

2 tablespoons balsamic vinegar

1 garlic clove, crushed

2 tablespoons hazelnut oil

4 tablespoons groundnut oil

sea salt and pepper

1 Mix together the marinade ingredients and place in a plastic container with the rabbit loins. Cover and leave to marinate in the refrigerator for 24 hours.

2 Blanch the green beans in boiling salted water for about 30 seconds. Drain, rinse under cold water and set aside.

3 To make the croûtons, toast one side of the French bread slices under a preheated grill and then place them, untoasted-side up, on a baking sheet. Beat together the butter and mustard and spread on the bread. Place under the grill until toasted to a golden colour. Transfer the croûtons to serving plates.

4 Mix together all the ingredients for the balsamic vinaigrette and arrange the salad leaves on top of the croûtons.

5 Heat the griddle pan and place the rabbit and green beans on it. Cook for 2–3 minutes, turn over, and cook for a further 2–3 minutes. Slice the griddled rabbit on the diagonal into long rounds. Arrange the rabbit and green beans on top of the salad leaves and drizzle over the vinaigrette. Serve immediately.

pork chops
with gingered apple and rosemary

Serves	**4**
Preparation time	**15** minutes
Cooking time	**30** minutes
Kcal	**687**
KJ	**2860**
Protein	**22** g
Fat	**50** g
CHO	**39** g

4 cooking or eating apples, peeled,
   cored and cut into 8 wedges

1 teaspoon rosemary leaves

2 tablespoons clear honey

½ tablespoon finely chopped fresh
   root ginger

2 tablespoons water

1 garlic clove, crushed and
   chopped

3 tablespoons olive oil

1 tablespoon sherry vinegar

2 teaspoons Dijon mustard

4 pork loin chops, bone removed

500 g/1 lb young parsnips, peeled
   and cut into thin lengths

25 g/1 oz melted butter

sea salt and pepper

1 Place the apples in a saucepan with the rosemary, honey, ginger and water. Cover and bring to the boil, then lower the heat and simmer for 10 minutes, until the apples are tender. Remove from the heat. Then mix the garlic, olive oil, vinegar and Dijon mustard in a small bowl.

2 Heat the griddle pan, add the chops and cook for 10 minutes on each side.

3 Meanwhile, brush the parsnips with melted butter, sprinkle with salt and pepper, and cook under a preheated hot grill for 10 minutes on each side.

4 To serve, pour the mustard dressing over the chops and serve with the gingered apple sauce and grilled parsnips.

This combination of comforting ingredients makes a memorable meal. The sauce can be made a few hours in advance and warmed up before serving.

lamb chops
with warm new potatoes

4	Serves
10 minutes	Preparation time
about **30** minutes	Cooking time
659	Kcal
2753	KJ
25 g	Protein
50 g	Fat
31 g	CHO

finely grated rind and juice of

  2 limes

8 tablespoons grapeseed oil

2 tablespoons chopped mint

4 lamb chops

750 g/1½ lb small new potatoes,

  halved lengthways

sea salt and pepper

mint leaves, to garnish

1 Combine the lime rind and juice and the oil, beating well with a whisk. Season with salt and pepper, add the chopped mint and whisk until evenly combined.

2 Heat the griddle pan. Put the lamb chops on the griddle and cook for 6 minutes on each side. Transfer to a warmed serving dish, cover and keep warm.

3 Place a layer of potato slices on the hot griddle and cook for 6 minutes on each side, reducing the heat as required. Remove and keep warm while cooking the remaining potato slices.

4 Toss the potatoes in the dressing, pile on to the serving dish and garnish with the mint.

Grapeseed oil is a pale, delicate, fairly neutral tasting oil which is extracted from grape pips. It is excellent for frying, dressings and for making mayonnaise.

thin steak
on a bed of hot leaves

Serves	**4**
Preparation time	**15** minutes
Cooking time	**10** minutes
Kcal	**423**
KJ	**1760**
Protein	**36** g
Fat	**30** g
CHO	**1** g

4 x 175 g/6 oz entrecôte steaks,
   trimmed

8 tablespoons olive oil

juice of 1 lemon

2 tablespoons red wine vinegar

250 g/8 oz mixed hot salad leaves,
   (e.g. rocket and watercress)

sea salt and pepper

1 Spread out a piece of clingfilm, place a steak in the middle and cover with another piece of clingfilm. Using a rolling pin or wooden mallet, gently beat the steak until it is at least twice its original size. Repeat with the remaining steaks.

2 Mix together the olive oil, lemon juice, red wine vinegar and season with salt and pepper. Pour over the leaves and toss well. Divide the salad leaves between 4 plates.

3 Heat the griddle pan until very hot. Season the steaks with salt and pepper on both sides, place on the griddle and flash-cook on both sides, just long enough to sear the meat. Place on the salad leaves and serve immediately.

Make sure that you flatten the steak out as thinly as possible and then just flash-cook on a very hot griddle pan. Hot salad leaves such as rocket have a spicy, peppery flavour.

sweet and sour
pork ribs

4	Serves
20 minutes, plus marinating	Preparation time
30 minutes	Cooking time
560	Kcal
2340	KJ
30 g	Protein
36 g	Fat
32 g	CHO

1 Combine the tomato ketchup, vinegar, sugar, garlic, ginger, pineapple and soy sauce in a saucepan and bring to the boil.

2 Blend the cornflour with the water and stir into the marinade mixture. Bring to the boil again, stirring until the mixture thickens.

1 kg/2 lb spare ribs, separated and cut to fit the griddle pan

marinade:

125 ml/4 fl oz tomato ketchup

1 tablespoon malt vinegar

3 tablespoons sugar

2 garlic cloves, crushed

1 teaspoon finely chopped fresh root ginger

1 tablespoon finely chopped pineapple

3 tablespoons soy sauce

1 tablespoon cornflour

3 tablespoons water

3 Place the ribs in the marinade and leave for at least 2 hours but preferably overnight.

4 Heat the griddle pan and place the ribs on the griddle. Griddle over a medium heat, turning constantly and brushing with lany remaining marinade, for 30 minutes, or until cooked through and crispy on the outside.

To blend or to slake is the method of mixing a starchy ingredient, such as flour, with a small quantity of liquid to form a smooth consistency.

fish

Griddling fish and shellfish is a quick and easy way to way to create really impressive meals. The distinctive griddle marks look fantastic on fish as well as adding to the flavour.

dishes

red snapper
and spicy tomato salsa

Serves	**4**
Preparation time	**20** minutes, plus marinating
Cooking time	**10** minutes
Kcal	**288**
KJ	**1212**
Protein	**37** g
Fat	**13** g
CHO	**6** g

4 x 175 g/6 oz red snapper fillets

lime wedges, to serve

sprigs of coriander, to garnish

spicy tomato salsa:

6 tomatoes, skinned, deseeded and chopped

1 bunch of spring onions, chopped

1 garlic clove, crushed and chopped

1 bunch of coriander, chopped

2 chillies, deseeded and diced

juice of 2 limes

1 ripe avocado, pitted and diced

2 tablespoons olive oil

sea salt and pepper

1 Combine all the salsa ingredients together, cover and set aside to marinate for at least 2–3 hours. If a smooth salsa is preferred, place all the ingredients in a food processor or blender and process.

2 Heat the griddle pan, put on the snapper fillets, skin-side down, and cook for 3–4 minutes. Turn and cook for a further 3 minutes, or until firm to the touch. Serve immediately with the salsa and lime wedges and garnish with sprigs of coriander.

There are many types of salsa, but this is a classic and very popular one. Make the salsa a few hours in advance to allow the flavours to blend together.

tuna steaks
with a quick tomato sauce

4	Serves
5 minutes	Preparation time
22 minutes	Cooking time
153	Kcal
644	KJ
25 g	Protein
5 g	Fat
3 g	CHO

4 x 125 g/4 oz tuna steaks

lime wedges, to serve

quick tomato sauce:

4 plum tomatoes

1 teaspoon garlic purée

1 tablespoon tomato purée

1 tablespoon chopped parsley

salt and pepper

1 To make the tomato sauce, put all the sauce ingredients into a blender or food processor and blend for 1 minute. Transfer to a saucepan and cook, uncovered, for 10 minutes.

2 Heat the griddle pan until it is very hot. Put on 2 of the tuna steaks and cook for 3 minutes on each side. Remove from the pan and keep warm. Repeat with the remaining tuna steaks.

3 Season the tomato sauce with salt and pepper and spoon over the cooked tuna. Serve with the lime wedges.

Be careful not to overcook the tuna steaks or they may become too dry. Alternatively, serve the steaks with the Savoury Salsa (see page 120).

mahi mahi
with wasabi–lime butter

Serves	**4**
Preparation time	**35** minutes, plus chilling
Cooking time	about **10** minutes
Kcal	**427**
KJ	**1775**
Protein	**32** g
Fat	**33** g
CHO	**0** g

125 g/4 oz butter at room
   temperature
grated rind and juice of 1 lime
2 teaspoons wasabi paste
4 x 175 g/6 oz mahi mahi, tuna or
   swordfish steaks
pepper

1 Place the butter, lime rind and juice and wasabi paste in a food processor or blender and blend well. Spoon the mixture on to greaseproof paper, wrap the paper round and roll into a sausage shape. Place in the refrigerator for 30 minutes until the wasibi-lime butter is firm.

2 Heat the griddle pan, and cook the fish for 4 minutes on each side. To make a criss-cross effect, cook the fish on one side for about 2 minutes on a high heat, then give the fish a quarter turn and cook for a further 2 minutes. Repeat for the other side. The fish is cooked when firm to the touch and charred.

3 Cut the butter into 8 equal slices. Top each piece of fish with 2 slices of butter. Season with pepper and serve immediately, with green vegetables and boiled white rice, if liked.

Mahi mahi is similar in texture to tuna and swordfish. It is sometimes called dorado because of its vibrant gold and jewel coloured skin. The wasabi butter also goes well with other fish and with chicken.

salmon
and courgette brochettes

4	Serves
15 minutes, plus marinating	Preparation time
about **5** minutes	Cooking time
650	Kcal
2695	KJ
39 g	Protein
54 g	Fat
2 g	CHO

750 g–1 kg/1½–2 lb salmon

   fillet, skinned and cut into

   2.5 cm/1 inch cubes

375 g/12 oz courgettes, cut into

1 cm/½ inch pieces

whole chives, to garnish

marinade:

8 tablespoons sunflower oil

2 tablespoons light sesame seed oil

2 tablespoons sesame seeds

1 garlic clove, crushed

1–2 tablespoons lime juice

pepper

to serve:

rocket

lime wedges

1 Combine all the marinade ingredients in a large bowl. Add the salmon and courgette pieces and toss well to coat completely. Cover and leave to marinate for about 30 minutes.

2 Heat the griddle pan. Thread the salmon and courgette pieces alternately on to 8 metal or wooden skewers. If using wooden, soak in cold water before use. Cook the kebabs for about 6 minutes, turning them frequently and brushing with the marinade to keep the fish and courgettes from drying out. The fish is cooked when it is just beginning to look milky. Do not overcook it or it will become dry and tough. Serve immediately on a bed of rocket with lime wedges, garnished with whole chives.

These kebabs are delicious served on mashed potatoes flavoured with olive oil, and with a salad dressed with the Lime and Sesame Dressing (see page 11). They can also be made with fresh tuna or swordfish.

griddled scallops
with smoked bacon

Serves	**4**
Preparation time	**5** minutes
Cooking time	**6** minutes
Kcal	**453**
KJ	**1883**
Protein	**33** g
Fat	**34** g
CHO	**49** g

6 fresh bay leaves

**12 large scallops, Scottish if
    possible**

**12 rashers of smoked streaky
    bacon, derinded**

250 g/8 oz mixed lettuce leaves

**½ recipe quantity Citrus Dressing
    (see page 121)**

lemon or lime wedges, to serve

1 Lay half a bay leaf on each scallop, then wrap them up tightly in a rasher of bacon. Heat the griddle pan and put on the wrapped scallops, seam-side down. Cook on both sides for 3 minutes, until the bacon is crispy and golden on the outside. The scallops should still be soft and juicy inside.

2 Toss the lettuce leaves in the citrus dressing, then arrange on 4 serving plates in mounds. Top with the griddled scallops and serve with lemon or lime wedges.

Scottish scallops are the best. They are dived for in the lochs and sold fresh the next day. They are not cheap, but they are well worth the money for their delicious taste.

scottish scallops
with sage

4	Serves
10 minutes	Preparation time
8 minutes	Cooking time
163	Kcal
680	KJ
17 g	Protein
9 g	Fat
3 g	CHO

1 Dry the scallops thoroughly with kitchen paper.

2 Heat the griddle pan, put on the scallops and cook on each side for 2–3 minutes. Add the sage leaves and cook until just wilting.

16 Scottish scallops

good bunch of sage leaves

3 tablespoons olive oil

1 tablespoon balsamic vinegar

sea salt and pepper

4 lemon wedges, to serve

3 Mix together the olive oil and the balsamic vinegar in a shallow dish. Remove the scallops and sage from the heat and toss well in the dressing. Season to taste with salt and pepper and serve immediately with lemon wedges.

Fresh sage leaves add a lovely subtle flavour and colour. This is a quick and simple dish, perfect for the busy host to serve as an impressive starter.

cod wrapped
in parma ham and cheese

Serves	**4**
Preparation time	about **20** minutes
Cooking time	**15–20** minutes
Kcal	**290**
KJ	**1223**
Protein	**44** g
Fat	**13** g
CHO	**0** g

4 x 175 g/6 oz cod fillets, skinned

4 thin slices of Gruyère cheese

4–8 bay leaves, depending on size

8 thin slices of Parma ham

sea salt and pepper

1 Heat the griddle pan. Season the cod fillets with salt and pepper to taste.

2 Trim any rind from the cheese and cut it to fit on top of the cod fillets. Place the cheese slices on the fish, then place the bay leaves on top of the cheese and neatly wrap the Parma ham around the cod fillets, securing the cheese and bay leaves.

3 Cook the wrapped cod on the griddle for 4-5 minutes on each side, taking care when turning each fillet. Serve with a leafy green salad, if liked.

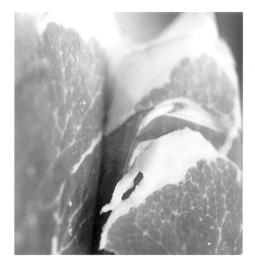

Emmenthal cheese can also be used for this recipe. Its smooth texture and mellow nutty flavour makes it ideal for cooking.

cod steaks
with mint pesto

4	Serves
10 minutes	Preparation time
8–10 minutes	Cooking time
250	Kcal
1050	KJ
29 g	Protein
15 g	Fat
1 g	CHO

1 Heat the griddle pan and put on the steaks and cook for 4 minutes on each side, until slightly charred and firm to the touch.

2 Place the pesto ingredients in a food processor or blender, season to taste with salt and pepper and process until smooth. Transfer to a small bowl.

3 Serve the cod steaks with a spoonful of pesto and with seasoned green vegetables. Serve with lime wedges.

4 x 175 g/6 oz cod steaks

1 lime, cut into wedges, to garnish

mint pesto:

6 tablespoons chopped mint

1 tablespoon chopped parsley

1 garlic clove, crushed and chopped

1 tablespoon grated Parmesan cheese

sea salt and pepper

Mint pesto is best served fresh as, although it will keep, it tends to lose its bright green colour and depth of flavour.

tuna salad niçoise

Serves	**4**
Preparation time	**30** minutes
Cooking time	**20** minutes
Kcal	**428**
KJ	**1791**
Protein	**33** g
Fat	**24** g
CHO	**22** g

375 g/12 oz skinless tuna

8 small potatoes, cooked and sliced

6 tomatoes, skinned and quartered

250 g/8 oz cooked French beans

1 red onion, sliced

1 Cos lettuce heart, cut into
    quarters

4 anchovy fillets, halved

4 hard-boiled eggs, sliced or
    quartered

8 black olives

1 tablespoon chopped flat leaf
    parsley

1 Heat the griddle pan and cook the tuna for 2 minutes on each side if you like it rare, or for about 4 minutes on each side if you like it well done. Remove and allow to cool for 5 minutes.

dressing:

1 tablespoon wine vinegar

juice of 1 lemon

4 tablespoons olive oil

1 garlic clove, crushed and
    chopped

1 teaspoon mustard

sea salt and pepper

2 Mix together the potatoes, tomatoes, French beans, onion and lettuce in a large salad bowl. Arrange the anchovy fillets, hard-boiled eggs and olives on top.

3 Process all the ingredients for the dressing in a blender, or place them in a screw-top jar and shake well to combine thoroughly.

4 Slice the tuna fillet and arrange it around the salad mixture. Spoon the dressing over the salad and garnish with chopped parsley.

Forget the tin of tuna in the cupboard and buy some fresh tuna to make this superb salad. Fresh tuna should be firm and red in colour.

sesame-crusted salmon

fillet salad

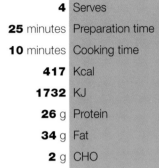

4	Serves
25 minutes	Preparation time
10 minutes	Cooking time
417	Kcal
1732	KJ
26 g	Protein
34 g	Fat
2 g	CHO

500 g/1 lb salmon fillet (middle is
   best)

2 egg whites, lightly beaten

1 tablespoon white sesame seeds

1 tablespoon black sesame seeds

2 bunches of watercress

1 frisée lettuce, divided into leaves

4 spring onions, cut into thin strips
   and placed in water

sea salt and pepper

1 Dry the salmon with kitchen paper, then dip it in the egg white. Mix the sesame seeds and salt and pepper to taste on a large plate. Roll the salmon in the sesame seeds and pat on the seeds all over to give a good even coating. Heat the griddle pan, put on the salmon and cook for about 2 minutes on each side for rare, or 5 minutes for well done.

dressing:

3 tablespoons white wine vinegar

5 tablespoons vegetable oil

1 tablespoon soy sauce

1 tablespoon sesame oil

1 teaspoon caster sugar

bunch of chopped chives

2 Process the dressing ingredients in a blender or place in a screw-top jar and shake well to combine. Toss the watercress and frisée in the dressing and arrange on a large serving dish.

3 Slice the salmon fillet with a sharp, thin-bladed knife and arrange on top of the salad. Drain the curled spring onions, dry on kitchen paper and sprinkle over the salmon.

The crust on this salmon makes it really special. The dressing is a must as it complements the slightly oriental salmon so well. This is a great dinner party dish, because it is not only easy to prepare, but also sensational both to look at and to eat.

tarragon-infused
sea bass fillets

Serves	**4**
Preparation time:	**5** minutes
Cooking time:	**6** minutes
Kcal	**224**
KJ	**940**
Protein	**34** g
Fat	**10** g
CHO	**0** g

4 x 175 g/6 oz sea bass fillets

1 large bunch of tarragon

2 tablespoons olive oil

juice of 1 lemon

sea salt and pepper

1 lemon, cut into wedges, to
  garnish

1 Heat the griddle pan, put on the sea bass, skin-side down, and cook for 3 minutes. Place a quarter of the tarragon on each fillet, pressing it into the fish. Turn the fish so that it is resting on the tarragon and cook for a further 3 minutes. Place the lemon wedges on the griddle and cook on each side for 1 minute.

2 To serve, drizzle the fillets with olive oil and lemon juice, and season to taste with salt and pepper. Garnish with the tarragon and griddled wedges of lemon.

This is a wonderful way to cook this most supreme of fish. It may seem odd to griddle the tarragon, but in this way all the flavours will be absorbed into the sea bass.

tuna

with rice noodles and ginger

4	Serves
15 minutes	Preparation time
about **25** minutes	Cooking time
487	Kcal
2040	KJ
34 g	Protein
14 g	Fat
54 g	CHO

1 Heat a little grapeseed oil in a small saucepan, and add the ginger, garlic, shallots, chilli and lemon grass. Heat gently, but do not allow to brown. Meanwhile, put on a large pan of water to boil for the rice noodles.

1 tablespoon grapeseed oil

5 cm/2 inch piece of fresh root ginger, peeled and finely diced

2 garlic cloves, chopped

2 shallots, finely chopped

1 green chilli, deseeded and finely chopped

1 stalk lemon grass, finely sliced

250 g/8 oz rice noodles

500 g/1 lb tuna fillet

grated rind and juice of 1 lime

2 tablespoons soy sauce

2 tablespoons sesame oil

1 bunch of coriander, chopped

1 lime, cut into 4 wedges, to serve

sprigs of coriander, to garnish

2 Heat the griddle pan and put on the tuna fillet. Cook for 1–2 minutes on each side over a medium to high heat, gradually turning the tuna so that all sides are charred. When cooked, place on a chopping board to rest for 3 minutes.

3 Plunge the noodles into the boiling water and cook according to packet instructions. Drain well and return to the pan. Add the cooked ginger mixture, and the lime rind and juice, soy sauce and sesame oil. Mix well, then cover and keep warm.

4 Place the lime wedges on the griddle and cook on each side for 1 minute. This will give them a lovely charred effect and warm the juice slightly. Add the chopped coriander to the rice noodles and mix well. Arrange the noodles in a large serving dish. Cut the tuna into 1 cm/½ inch slices and arrange on top of the rice noodles. Serve immediately with the griddled wedges of lime, garnished with the coriander,

The tuna is meant to be pink and rare, but if this is not to your liking just griddle for longer. In California, the tuna is barely cooked: this is delicious, but the tuna must be very fresh.

salmon steaks
with teriyaki sauce

Serves	**4**
Preparation time	**15** minutes
Cooking time	about **20** minutes
Kcal	**414**
KJ	**1725**
Protein	**33** g
Fat	**27** g
CHO	**12** g

1 To make the teriyaki sauce, place all the sauce ingredients in a small saucepan and bring to the boil. Simmer fast for 10 minutes or until reduced to a thick, glossy sauce. Set aside to cool for about 5 minutes before using.

2 Heat the griddle pan over a medium heat and put on the salmon steaks. Cook for about 4 minutes on each side, until charred and firm to the touch.

4 x 175 g/6 oz salmon steaks

4 little gem lettuces, quartered lengthways

teriyaki sauce:

1 tablespoon sunflower oil

1 tablespoon sesame oil

6 tablespoons teriyaki sauce

2 tablespoons rice or white wine vinegar

juice of 1 lime

2 tablespoons clear honey

3 Arrange the pieces of lettuce on 4 plates. Place the salmon steaks on top of the lettuce. Spoon the sauce over the salmon and let it run over the salad. Serve at once.

Japanese teriyaki sauce is delicious and goes well with this griddled salmon as well as griddled meat such as rump steak.

griddled cod
with sage and lemon oil

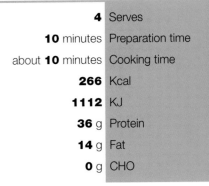

4	Serves
10 minutes	Preparation time
about **10** minutes	Cooking time
266	Kcal
1112	KJ
36 g	Protein
14 g	Fat
0 g	CHO

1 Dry the cod fillets with kitchen paper and season to taste with salt and pepper. Place a sage leaf on each piece of cod.

2 Wrap the slices of Parma ham around the cod fillets, covering them completely.

4 x 175g/6 oz cod fillets, skinned

4 sage leaves

8 slices Parma ham, finely sliced

4 tablespoons lemon oil
   (see below)

sea salt and pepper

3 Heat the griddle pan. Put the fish on the griddle and cook for 4 minutes on each side. Serve drizzled with the lemon oil and accompanied by mixed vegetables or noodles.

Lemon oil can be purchased from delicatessens and specialist food stores. To make it at home, take a small bottle of olive oil, remove the rind from 2 lemons (preferably unwaxed) in large long strips, and place the rind in the olive oil. Reseal and allow to infuse for 1 week.

red mullet
with walnut and parsley pesto

Serves	**4**
Preparation time	**10** minutes
Cooking time	**6** minutes
Kcal	**352**
KJ	**1466**
Protein	**30** g
Fat	**25** g
CHO	**1** g

1 To make the walnut and parsley pesto, place all the pesto ingredients in a food processor or blender, and process until fairly smooth. Season to taste.

4 x 150 g/5 oz red mullet fillets, descaled

1 lemon, cut into 4 wedges, to serve

walnut and parsley pesto:

50 g/2 oz walnut pieces, toasted

4 spring onions, chopped

1 garlic clove, chopped

2 tablespoons chopped parsley

4 tablespoons extra virgin olive oil

sea salt and pepper

2 Heat the griddle pan, put on the fish fillets skin side-down and cook for 3 minutes on both sides. The fish should be slightly charred on the outside and firm to the touch. Serve with a generous spoonful of the pesto and serve with lemon wedges.

If you can't find this size of red mullet fillet, serve two smaller fillets per person.

rainbow trout
with ground almond dressing

4	Serves
10 minutes	Preparation time
25 minutes	Cooking time
510	Kcal
2118	KJ
36 g	Protein
40 g	Fat
2 g	CHO

1 Rinse the trout and pat dry with kitchen paper. Heat the griddle pan, put on the trout and cook on each side for 8 minutes, carefully turning the fish with a palette knife. The skin should be charred.

2 To make the dressing, place the almonds in a small saucepan over medium heat and stir constantly until lightly browned. Remove from the heat and add the oil, lemon juice, salt and pepper to taste and chopped parsley. Stir well and return to the heat for 2 minutes.

3 Serve the trout with the almond dressing poured over and garnish with sprigs of parsley.

4 rainbow trout, about 300 g/10 oz each, heads and tails left on

125 g/4 oz ground almonds

6 tablespoons olive oil

juice of 1 lemon

2 tablespoons chopped parsley

sea salt and pepper

sprigs of parsley, to garnish

Pink-fleshed rainbow trout is reasonably priced and readily available; the sharp, lemony flavour of the almond dressing complements the trout particularly well.

squid and prawns
with spicy chilli sauce

Serves	**4**
Preparation time	**10** minutes
Cooking time	about **20** minutes
Kcal	**274**
KJ	**1140**
Protein	**25** g
Fat	**15** g
CHO	**9** g

375 g/12 oz prepared squid, opened out

12 raw king or tiger prawns

chilli sauce:

2 red peppers

2 fresh red chillies

2 tablespoons sherry vinegar

3 tablespoons chopped oregano

5 tablespoons olive oil

2 shallots, finely chopped

juice of ½ lemon

sea salt and pepper

1 To make the sauce, heat the griddle pan, slice the bottom off the peppers, then slice down the sides into 4–5 flat pieces, leaving the seeds on the core. Slice the chillies into wide, flat pieces, discarding the seeds. Place the peppers skin-side down on the griddle pan and cook for about 10 minutes until the skins are charred and blistered. Remove and cook the chillies in the same way. Place the peppers and chillies in a small dish, cover with clingfilm and leave to cool.

2 Skin the peppers and chillies and place in a food processor or blender with the vinegar. Process until smooth, season to taste with salt and pepper and pour into a small saucepan.

3 Cut the squid in half, then score in a criss-cross pattern with a sharp knife. Heat the griddle pan and cook the prawns on each side for 2 minutes. Remove and cook the squid on each side for 1–2 minutes. They will curl up, so use a palette knife to hold them flat. Half each piece once cooked.

4 Warm up the chilli sauce, adding the oregano, oil, shallots and lemon juice. Toss the prawns and squid in the warm chilli sauce and serve with fresh pasta.

Small, young squid are the most tender. The trick is not to overcook them, as they become tough if cooked for too long.

aromatic tilapia
in banana leaf parcels

4	Serves
20 minutes	Preparation time
about **20** minutes	Cooking time
244	Kcal
1018	KJ
31 g	Protein
10 g	Fat
7 g	CHO

10 shallots or 2 Spanish onions,
   finely chopped

3 garlic cloves, finely chopped

5–10 small red and green chillies,
   deseeded and sliced

2 handfuls of basil leaves

2 spring onions, chopped

light soy sauce, to taste

4 pieces of banana leaf or strong
   aluminium foil for wrapping

4 x 250 g/8 oz tilapia or red
   snapper fillets

juice of 1 lime

vegetable oil, for greasing

sea salt

1 lime, cut into wedges, to serve

1 Mix together the shallots and garlic with the chillies, basil, spring onions and salt. Moisten with a little soy sauce.

2 Soften the banana leaves (see tip below) or, if using foil, lightly grease the inner side of the foil. The banana leaves should be slightly longer than the fish and square in shape.

3 Put a whole fish on each banana leaf, squeeze the lime juice over it and spoon the herb mixture around it on both sides and in the cavity. Roll up the leaves and fold the ends into points. Secure with cocktail sticks.

4 Heat the griddle pan. Steam for 10–15 minutes, then griddle over a low heat for 2 minutes on each side until the leaves turn brown. If using aluminium foil, it can be put straight into the griddle pan and cooked over a low heat for 20 minutes or until the flesh is firm and opaque.

5 Serve the fish in the parcels so guests can appreciate the aroma as the parcels are opened. Serve with lime wedges.

Softening banana leaves makes them easier to bend and wrap. To soften, put them into a bowl and pour over boiling water; then drain. Alternatively, warm carefully over a hot electric stove or a gas ring.

salmon fillets
with pesto and lemon rice

Serves	**4**
Preparation time	**15** minutes
Cooking time	about **20** minutes
Kcal	**544**
KJ	**2257**
Protein	**31** g
Fat	**40** g
CHO	**16** g

75 g/3 oz long-grain rice

grated rind and juice of 1 lemon

4 x 150 g/5 oz salmon fillets

50 g/2 oz butter

basil leaves, to garnish

pesto:

1 garlic clove, chopped

15 g/½ oz basil leaves

15 g/½ oz pine nuts

3 tablespoons extra virgin olive oil

1 tablespoon freshly grated
   Parmesan cheese

sea salt and pepper

1 Bring a large saucepan of water to the boil, add the rice and the lemon rind, and return to the boil. Simmer gently for 10–12 minutes until the rice is cooked.

2 Meanwhile, to make the pesto, place all the ingredients in a food processor or blender and process until smooth.

3 Heat the griddle pan. Remove any remaining bones from the salmon with a pair of tweezers, and pat dry with kitchen paper. Place the fillets on the hot griddle, skin-side down, and cook for 3 minutes. Turn and cook for another 2–3 minutes until cooked through and firm to the touch.

4 Drain the rice and immediately stir in the lemon juice and butter. Season to taste. Serve the salmon fillets on a bed of rice with the pesto sauce spooned over and. garnished with basil leaves.

The high oil content of salmon means that it cooks very well on a griddle pan.

thai fish
and prawn cakes

4–6 as a starter	Serves
40 minutes	Preparation time
about **25** minutes	Cooking time
226	Kcal
950	KJ
26 g	Protein
8 g	Fat
12 g	CHO

1 Place the fish, prawns and red curry paste in a food processor and process for a short time until a rough paste is formed.

2 Transfer the fish paste into a large bowl and add all the remaining ingredients. Mix with a wooden spoon until thoroughly combined. Divide the mixture into 24 rounds and neatly roll into small cakes.

400 g/13 oz fish fillets (e.g. salmon, trout, coley), skin and bones removed

125 g/4 oz raw prawns, shelled and deveined

3 tablespoons Thai red curry paste

125 g/4 oz green beans, finely chopped into rings

250 g/8 oz potato, cooked and mashed

8 Thai basil leaves, chopped

4 kaffir lime leaves, finely chopped or 1 tablespoon finely chopped lime rind

1 egg yolk

2 teaspoons sea salt

oil, for frying

Sweet and Hot Dipping Sauce (see page 119), to serve

3 Heat the griddle pan and brush lightly with oil. Cook the fish cakes in batches for 4 minutes on each side. Keep the cooked batches warm as the remaining cakes are being griddled.

4 Serve with small individual bowls of the dipping sauce.

The fiery temperature of the Thai red curry paste depends on the number of chillies used.

salads anc

Griddled ingredients can be simply tossed with a tasty home-made dressing to create substantial salads or delicious accompaniments for other griddled food.

dressings

warmed butternut
squash and sunshine salad

Serves	**4**
Preparation time	**10** minutes
Cooking time	**40** minutes
Kcal	**228**
KJ	**945**
Protein	**5** g
Fat	**20** g
CHO	**7** g

1 small butternut squash, halved, deseeded and cut into 2.5 cm/1 inch wedges

175 g/6 oz baby sweetcorn cobs

2 yellow courgettes, cut diagonally into 1 cm/½ inch pieces

50 g/2 oz toasted pine nuts

1 bunch of chopped oregano

4 tablespoons lemon oil

sea salt and pepper

1 Heat the griddle pan, add the squash in batches and cook until soft all over, about 6 minutes on each side. To test, insert the tip of a knife into the thickest part of the squash – it should go in easily. Repeat until all the squash is cooked, and arrange on a large warmed serving dish.

2 Add the baby sweetcorn cobs to the griddle pan and cook for 6 minutes, moving constantly, until they are lightly charred. Arrange on the same dish as the squash. Add the courgette pieces and cook for 2 minutes on each side, then add to the other vegetables.

3 Sprinkle the pine nuts, chopped oregano, salt and pepper over the salad and lastly drizzle the lemon oil over. Serve immediately with crusty bread, if liked.

Butternut squash are also good roasted, boiled or mashed. Lemon oil can be purchased or made at home (see tip on page 91).

griddled beetroot
and wild rice salad with feta

4	Serves
35 minutes	Preparation time
8–10 minutes	Cooking time
400	Kcal
1670	KJ
10 g	Protein
23 g	Fat
40 g	CHO

250 g/8 oz beetroot, ready cooked, cut into quarters

4 red onions, cut into wedges

300 g/10 oz mixed wild and basmati rice, cooked

1 bunch of mint, leaves only, chopped, a few sprigs reserved for garnish

125 g/4 oz feta cheese, cut into rough cubes

dressing:

2 tablespoons balsamic vinegar

6 tablespoons olive oil

pinch of sugar

sea salt and pepper

1 Heat the griddle pan. Cook the beetroot and red onions for 2 minutes on each side. Transfer to a large bowl.

2 To make the dressing, mix together the vinegar, oil and sugar and season to taste with salt and pepper. Add the cooked rice, chopped mint and the dressing to the bowl and mix together gently. Served sprinkled with the feta and garnished with the mint sprigs.

Feta is a soft, white crumbly Greek cheese originally made from ewe's milk or goat's milk; it is now often made from cow's milk.

asparagus
with tarragon and lemon dressing

Serves	**4**
Preparation time	**15** minutes
Cooking time	**5** minutes
Kcal	**250**
KJ	**1035**
Protein	**5** g
Fat	**24** g
CHO	**5** g

500 g/1 lb asparagus

125 g/4 oz rocket or other green
   leaves

2 spring onions, finely sliced

4 radishes, thinly sliced

sea salt and pepper

tarragon and lemon dressing:

2 tablespoons tarragon vinegar

finely grated rind of 1 lemon

¼ teaspoon Dijon mustard

pinch of sugar

1 tablespoon chopped tarragon

5 tablespoons olive oil

sea salt and pepper

to garnish:

chopped herbs (e.g. dill, tarragon,
   parsley, chervil)

thin strips of lemon rind

1 To make the dressing, put all the dressing ingredients in a screw-top jar and shake well.

2 Heat the griddle pan. Place the asparagus on the griddle in a single layer and cook for about 5 minutes, turning occasionally. The asparagus should be tender when pierced with the tip of a sharp knife, and lightly browned in patches. Transfer to a shallow dish and season to taste with salt and pepper. Pour over the dressing and toss gently. Set aside to cool for 5 minutes.

3 Arrange the rocket or green leaves on a platter, sprinkle the spring onions and radishes over the top and arrange the asparagus in the middle of the leaves. Garnish with chopped herbs and thin strips of lemon rind. Serve with bread or as an accompaniment to a main dish.

Trim the ends of each asparagus stalk by cutting it across at a sharp angle. Make the cut just where the lovely, bright green colour starts to fade into a dull green.

mixed mung bean
salad

4	Serves
10 minutes, plus cooling	Preparation time
about **40** minutes	Cooking time
85	Kcal
358	KJ
4 g	Protein
4 g	Fat
10 g	CHO

1 Drain the mung beans, then put them into a saucepan with fresh water and bring to the boil. Boil for 15 minutes, drain, and rinse under cold water. Leave to cool.

2 Heat the griddle pan. Slice the aubergine in half lengthways and griddle for 3–4 minutes on each side. Add the red pepper and griddle for 3–4 minutes. Leave to cool slightly, then cut into pieces.

300 g/10 oz mung beans, soaked

1 aubergine

1 red pepper, cored, deseeded and
   cut into flat pieces

2 beef tomatoes, skinned

1 bunch of chives, chopped

1 tablespoon soy sauce

1 tablespoon sesame oil

juice of 2 limes

sea salt and pepper

3 Slice the tomatoes into slim wedges and mix with the aubergines, red pepper and mung beans. Add the chopped chives.

4 Add the soy sauce, sesame oil and lime juice. Season to taste with salt and pepper and mix again. Serve on its own or as an accompaniment to griddled chicken or fish.

Mung beans are one of the smallest beans and are so healthy and nutritious. They add a lovely olive green colour, crunchy texture and fresh flavour to salads, sandwiches and stir-fries.

bean salad
with griddled onions

Serves	**4**
Preparation time	**20** minutes
Cooking time	**1** hour using dried beans, **20** minutes using canned beans
Kcal	**522**
KJ	**2180**
Protein	**18** g
Fat	**28** g
CHO	**52** g

300 g/10 oz dried cannellini beans, soaked overnight, or 500 g/1 lb canned beans, drained

3 red or white onions, cut into wedges, root ends intact

flat leaf parsley, to garnish

1 Drain the soaked beans and place in a saucepan. Cover with plenty of water and bring to the boil. Boil rapidly for 10 minutes, then lower the heat and simmer for 40–50 minutes, or until tender. Drain in a colander, rinse under cold running water, and drain again. Transfer to a bowl and set aside to cool. If using canned beans, rinse these well.

dressing:

150 ml/¼ pint olive oil

5 tablespoons lemon juice

2 garlic cloves, crushed and chopped

2 tablespoons finely chopped flat leaf parsley

pinch of English mustard powder

pinch of sugar

sea salt and pepper

2 Heat the griddle pan. Place the onions on the griddle and cook for about 4 minutes on each side, or until they are charred. If they are charring too much, reduce the heat. Remove from the heat and set aside on a board to allow the onions to cool .

3 To prepare the dressing, whisk together all the ingredients in a bowl, or place them in a screw-top jar and shake well to combine.

4 Place the onions in a large bowl, pour over the dressing and mix in the beans. Transfer to a serving dish and garnish with chopped flat leaf parsley.

This makes a lovely colourful salad, with an interesting texture. Bean salads often get left at parties because they don't have enough taste, but this one is delicious. The onion wedges are left attached at the root end, which helps to hold them together.

red pepper
and chickpea salad

4	Serves
10 minutes, plus overnight soaking	Preparation time
about **1** hour	Cooking time
270	Kcal
1134	KJ
11 g	Protein
13 g	Fat
30 g	CHO

1 Cook the chickpeas in unsalted boiling water for about 45 minutes or until tender.

2 Heat the griddle pan. Add the peppers to the griddle and cook for about 10 minutes, turning frequently, until the skins blacken and blister. Hold the peppers under cold running water, then using a sharp knife, peel off the skins. Cut the peppers in half, core, deseed and cut into slices.

175 g/6 oz dried chickpeas, soaked
  overnight and drained

3 red peppers

12 black olives, pitted

2 tablespoons chopped coriander

orange dressing:

3 tablespoons sunflower oil

½ teaspoon grated orange rind

2 tablespoons orange juice

1 garlic clove, crushed

sea salt and pepper

3 To make the dressing, mix together the sunflower oil, orange rind and juice and garlic in a large bowl. Season to taste with salt and pepper.

4 Drain the chickpeas and toss in the orange dressing while they are still hot. Set aside to cool.

5 Stir in the peppers, olives and coriander. Turn into a serving dish.

To speed up this recipe, canned chickpeas can be used. Drain the chickpeas and rinse well under cold running water.

charred leeks
with honey and sesame vinaigrette

Serves	**4**
Preparation time	**10** minutes
Cooking time	about **5** minutes
Kcal	**345**
KJ	**1430**
Protein	**5** g
Fat	**31** g
CHO	**14** g

16 leeks, preferably young and small, trimmed, and cut in half lengthways

honey and sesame vinaigrette:

2 tablespoons clear honey

2 tablespoons white wine vinegar

125 ml/4 fl oz groundnut oil, plus extra for brushing

1 tablespoon sesame oil

sea salt and pepper

2 tablespoons chopped chives

to garnish:

4 tablespoons toasted sesame seeds

chive flowers

1 Heat the griddle pan and place the leeks on it cut-side up. Brush the leeks with a little oil and cook, in batches, for about 2 minutes until just tender. Remove and put on to plates.

2 To make the honey and sesame vinaigrette, combine the honey, vinegar, groundnut and sesame oils and the chives in a small bowl. Season to taste with salt and pepper. Alternatively, place all the ingredients in a screw-top jar and shake well.

3 Drizzle the leeks with the vinaigrette and sprinkle over the sesame seeds and garnish with the chive flowers.

To toast sesame seeds, put them into a dry pan over a moderate heat and stir constantly with a spoon or shake the pan until they are lightly browned.

griddled pear
and spinach salad

4	Serves
10 minutes	Preparation time
7 minutes	Cooking time
520	Kcal
2164	KJ
18 g	Protein
38 g	Fat
28 g	CHO

1 Cut each pear into quarters and remove the core, then slice each quarter in half. Heat the griddle pan. Place the slices of pear on the griddle and cook for 1 minute on each side. Remove from the pan and sprinkle with the lemon juice.

2 Pile the spinach on a large platter or 4 serving plates and arrange the pears on top. Sprinkle with the walnuts and crumbled Stilton and spoon the walnut oil over the salad. Serve immediately.

4 pears

4 tablespoons lemon juice

250 g/8 oz baby spinach

4 chopped walnuts

250 g/8 oz blue Stilton cheese,
  crumbled

4 tablespoons walnut oil

Blue Stilton is made from pasteurized cow's milk and is ripened for 3–4 months. It has a moist, crumbly texture, blue-green veining and a rich, tangy flavour.

smoky new potato
salad with mustard mayonnaise

Serves **4**

Preparation time **30** minutes

Cooking time **4** minutes

Kcal **652**

KJ **2697**

Protein **6** g

Fat **61** g

CHO **20** g

470 g/15 oz new potatoes, cooked
and cut in half

8 anchovies, rinsed and drained

2 tablespoons capers

chive flowers or nasturtiums,
to garnish

**mustard
mayonnaise:**

3 egg yolks

1 tablespoons white wine vinegar

2 tablespoons wholegrain mustard

300 ml/½ pint olive oil

1 tablespoon water

1 tablespoon lemon juice

sea salt and pepper

1 Heat the griddle pan and cook the potatoes for 2 minutes on each side, then place them in a large bowl with the anchovies and capers.

2 To make the mustard mayonnaise, whisk together the egg yolks, vinegar and mustard and season to taste with salt and pepper. Add the oil drop by drop, whisking continuously by hand or in a blender. Once the emulsion has formed the oil can be added more quickly. When all the oil is added, stir in the water and lemon juice; taste and adjust seasoning.

3 Gently mix the mustard mayonnaise with the potatoes and mix well. Serve garnished with the chive flowers or nasturtiums.

To prepare the new potatoes, boil them for 10–15 minutes, until just soft, before cooking in the griddle pan.

smoked chicken
and fruit salad

8	Serves
25 minutes	Preparation time
116	Kcal
485	KJ
11 g	Protein
5 g	Fat
6 g	CHO

2 pears, peeled, cored and sliced

lemon juice, for sprinkling

1 lettuce, shredded

2 celery sticks, chopped

1 red pepper, cored, deseeded and
   sliced

25 g/1 oz walnut halves

75 g/3 oz green grapes, peeled,
   halved and deseeded

250 g/8 oz smoked chicken,
   skinned, boned and cut into strips

tarragon sprigs, to garnish

low-fat dressing:

2 tablespoons low-fat natural
   yogurt

2 tablespoons low-fat mayonnaise

2 tablespoons grated cucumber

1 teaspoon grated onion

½ teaspoon chopped tarragon

sea salt and pepper

1 Heat the griddle pan. Place the slices of pear on the griddle and cook for 1 minute on each side. Remove from the pan and sprinkle with the lemon juice.

2 In a large salad bowl, mix the lettuce with the celery, red pepper, walnuts, grapes, pear slices and smoked chicken.

3 To make the low-fat dressing, mix the yogurt with the mayonnaise, cucumber, onion and tarragon. Blend well and season to taste with salt and pepper.

4 Just before serving, spoon the dressing over the salad and toss well to mix. Garnish with a few sprigs of fresh tarragon.

Any leftover smoked chicken will keep well and can be used in sandwiches. Use the bones to flavour stock.

italian-style
chicken salad with croûtons

Serves	**4**
Preparation time	**10** minutes
Cooking time	**15** minutes
Kcal	**560**
KJ	**2322**
Protein	**25** g
Fat	**46** g
CHO	**14** g

2 skinless boneless chicken breasts

1 Cos lettuce, torn to pieces

handful of basil leaves, roughly torn

3 slices ciabatta or white country bread, cubed and fried in oil

75 g/3 oz Parmesan cheese

dressing:

1 garlic clove, crushed and chopped

150 ml/¼ pint olive oil

3 anchovy fillets, roughly chopped

juice of ½ lemon

1 teaspoon English mustard powder

1 egg yolk

pepper

1 Heat the griddle pan. Place the chicken on the hot griddle and cook for 5 minutes on each side.

2 To make the dressing, put the garlic, olive oil, anchovies, lemon juice, mustard and egg yolk into a blender, season with pepper and mix until blended.

3 Put the lettuce into a large bowl, pour in the dressing and toss well. Then arrange the lettuce on serving plates and sprinkle with torn basil leaves and the croûtons.

4 Slice the chicken into long lengths and place on top of the lettuce. Shave the Parmesan on to the chicken with a vegetable peeler or grater and serve.

It is best to buy Parmesan cheese in a block and grate or shave it as required.

griddled fennel
with lemon and lime

4	Serves
10 minutes	Preparation time
4 minutes	Cooking time
327	Kcal
1353	KJ
15 g	Protein
29 g	Fat
2 g	CHO

1 Heat the griddle pan and cook the fennel for 2 minutes on each side then place them in a large bowl. Add the grated Parmesan, garlic, lemon and lime juices and olive oil and season to taste with salt and pepper.

2 large fennel bulbs, halved and sliced thinly, keeping the core intact

150 g/5 oz Parmesan cheese, grated, plus extra shavings, to garnish

1 garlic clove, crushed

juice of 2 lemons

juice of 2 limes

6 tablespoons olive oil

sea salt and pepper

2 Spoon the dressed fennel on to serving plates and garnish with the reserved Parmesan shavings. Serve as a vegetarian starter with crusty bread to mop up the juices, or as an accompaniment to a main dish.

Fennel is low in calories and rich in vitamins A and E. It has a pronounced aniseed flavour and is delicious griddled.

oriental marinade

Serves **4**

Preparation time **2** minutes

Kcal **44**

KJ **185**

Protein **2** g

Fat **0** g

CHO **10** g

4 tablespoons light soy sauce

2 tablespoons clear honey

2 tablespoons rice vinegar or rice
wine (or white wine vinegar)

1 tablespoon tomato purée

1 garlic clove, crushed

2.5 cm/1 inch piece of fresh root
ginger, peeled and grated

2 teaspoons Chinese five-spice
powder

1 Put all the ingredients in to a screw-top jar and shake vigorously until well combined. Alternatively, place all the ingredients in a small bowl and whisk with a fork.

A versatile marinade for lamb, pork or beef kebabs, chicken and duck skewers and even vegetable brochettes. It can be brushed on whilst cooking or, for a fuller flavour, used in advance to marinate the meat or poultry.

tomatoes
à la provençale

4 Serves
10 minutes Preparation time
about **20** minutes Cooking time
346 Kcal
1447 KJ
6 g Protein
24 g Fat
29 g CHO

1 Heat the griddle pan. Place the tomatoes cut-side down on the griddle and cook for 4 minutes on each side. Transfer them to a shallow, heatproof dish cut-side up and season with salt and pepper and sprinkle with sugar.

2 In a food processor, or using a pestle and mortar, blend together the breadcrumbs, parsley, garlic, lemon rind and salt and pepper to taste. Spoon the crumbs over the tomatoes and generously drizzle with the olive oil.

3 Place the tomatoes under a preheated grill for 3–4 minutes until the breadcrumbs are golden. Serve at room temperature on a bed of rocket leaves.

5 ripe plum tomatoes, halved

5 ripe yellow tomatoes, halved

5 pinches of sugar

150 g/5 oz fresh breadcrumbs

1 bunch of flat leaf parsley, leaves only

4 garlic cloves, chopped

thinly pared rind of 1 lemon, chopped

8 tablespoons olive oil

sea salt and pepper

125 g/4 oz rocket leaves, to serve

This is a great vegetarian dish and should be served with bread to mop up the juices. It is also an excellent accompaniment to griddled meats.

king prawn
and bacon salad

Serves	**4**
Preparation time	**15** minutes
Preparation time	about **5** minutes
Kcal	**317**
KJ	**1314**
Protein	**16** g
Fat	**26** g
CHO	**5** g

250 g/8 oz sugar snap peas or
   mangetout
6 rashers of rindless smoked
   streaky bacon
12 cooked king prawns, peeled
about 250 g/8 oz mixed salad
   leaves (e.g. red oakleaf,
   watercress, lamb's lettuce, four
   seasons, rocket)
2 spring onions, shredded
sea salt and pepper
1 quantity Tarragon and Lemon
   Dressing (see page 102)

1 Add the sugar snap peas or mangetout to a saucepan of boiling water and cook for 1 minute, then drain in a colander and cool under cold running water. Drain thoroughly and place in a large bowl.

2 Heat the griddle pan to medium hot. Cut the bacon rashers in half and wrap a half rasher around each prawn. Place on the griddle and cook for about 4 minutes, turning once, until the bacon is crisp and the prawns are hot.

3 Meanwhile, arrange the mixed salad leaves on 4 individual serving plates.

4 Add the cooked prawns and any cooking juices from the griddle pan to the sugar snap peas or mangetout with the spring onions. Pour over the dressing and season to taste with salt and pepper. (Go easy on the salt as the bacon and prawns are naturally salty.) Toss gently to mix all the ingredients together.

5 Arrange the prawns and vegetables on top of the salad leaves and serve at once.

For a stunning cocktail nibble, serve the griddled prawns wrapped in bacon and skewered with a cocktail stick. Increase the quantities according to the number of your guests.

lobster salad
with mango and chilli

4	Serves
20 minutes	Preparation time
about **10** minutes	Cooking time
449	Kcal
1887	KJ
24 g	Protein
12 g	Fat
62 g	CHO

4 lobster tails, halved lengthways

oil, for brushing

2 mangoes, peeled and cubed

500 g/1 lb rice sticks, soaked for
30 minutes in warm water and
drained

sea salt and pepper

chopped coriander, to garnish

dressing:

1 red chilli, deseeded and finely
chopped

2.5 cm/1 inch piece of fresh root
ginger, peeled and grated

juice of 1 lime

3 tablespoons groundnut oil

1 Mix the dressing ingredients together in a bowl; taste and adjust the seasoning; set aside.

2 Heat the griddle pan. Place the lobster tails on the griddle pan and cook for 5 minutes on each side until the shell turns bright pink and the flesh white and griddled. If liked, remove the flesh from the shell and cut it into bite-sized chunks.

3 To serve, mix the lobster meat, mangoes and rice sticks with the dressing and sprinkle with chopped coriander to garnish.

Cooked lobsters are available fresh or frozen from most large supermarkets. If using frozen lobsters, defrost well before cooking.

pepper and rice
salad with omelette ribbons

Serves	**4**
Preparation time	**25** minutes
Cooking time	about **15** minutes
Kcal	**293**
KJ	**1224**
Protein	**9** g
Fat	**16** g
CHO	**30** g

2 red peppers, halved, cored and
  deseeded

1 yellow pepper, halved, cored and
  deseeded

1 onion, cut into quarters, root ends
  intact

250 g/8 oz cooked rice (white,
  brown or a mixture of both)

sea salt and pepper

fresh herbs, to garnish

omelette:

3 eggs

2 tablespoons chopped herbs (e.g.
  parsley, dill, chives, chervil)

1 teaspoon light oil

dressing:

4 tablespoons half-fat crème
  fraîche

2 tablespoons olive oil

1 tablespoon white wine vinegar

1 Heat the griddle pan. Place the peppers and onion on the griddle and cook for about 10 minutes, until the peppers are blistered and blackened all over. Turn the onion wedges occasionally if necessary, but let them char a little. Remove the onions from the griddle and set aside to cool on a plate. Transfer the peppers to a bowl, cover with several layers of kitchen paper and set aside.

2 When cool enough to handle, rub off the charred skin from the peppers, and cut them into thin strips. Chop the onion. Combine the peppers and onion in a bowl. Add the rice, season with salt and pepper and toss lightly.

3 To make the omelette, lightly beat the eggs in a bowl with the herbs and a little salt and pepper. Heat the oil in a large frying pan, pour in the egg mixture and cook over a moderate heat. While the surface is still slightly creamy, slide the omelette on to a board and roll it up like a Swiss roll. Set aside to cool.

4 To make the dressing, stir all the dressing ingredients together in a small bowl. To serve, pile the rice mixture on to individual serving plates. Slice the omelette roll and arrange the ribbons on top of the salad. Drizzle the dressing over and garnish with fresh herbs.

salad tiède
with kidney, bacon and egg

4	Serves
10 minutes	Preparation time
about **15** minutes	Cooking time
436	Kcal
1812	KJ
23 g	Protein
38 g	Fat
1 g	CHO

1 Put a pan of water on to boil and add the vinegar. When it is boiling, crack in the eggs and poach for 3 minutes or until opaque but still soft in the middle.

1 tablespoon vinegar

4 small eggs

250 g/8 oz bacon, sliced into
  lardons

175 g/6 oz lambs' kidneys,
  (about 2), trimmed, cored and
  sliced

250 g/8 oz lamb's lettuce, washed

2 Heat the griddle pan. Cook the bacon until crispy then add the kidneys and cook for 1 minute on each side. Meanwhile, arrange the lamb's lettuce on 4 plates. Gently spoon the bacon and kidneys over the lettuce.

dressing:

4 tablespoons sherry vinegar

2 tablespoons hazelnut oil

sea salt and pepper

3 Deglaze the pan with the sherry vinegar and then pour the dressing over the salads. Drizzle over the hazelnut oil and top each salad with a poached egg. Sprinkle with sea salt and pepper.

To deglaze a pan of any congealed cooking juices or glaze, add liquid and bring to a boil, stirring and scraping constantly. The deglazed juices can be used as a dressing or added to a sauce.

hot papaya
and griddled pepper salsa

Makes	**500** g/**1** lb
Preparation time	**10** minutes, plus chilling
Cooking time	**10** minutes
Kcal	**700**
KJ	**2919**
Protein	**7** g
Fat	**46** g
CHO	**70** g

1 Heat the griddle pan. Add the peppers to the pan and cook for about 10 minutes, turning frequently, until the skins blacken and blister. Hold the peppers under cold running water, then using a sharp knife, peel off the skins. Cut into 5 mm/¼ inch dice.

2 red peppers, cored and deseeded

juice of 1–2 limes

4 tablespoons light olive oil

¼ teaspoon balsamic vinegar

**2 ripe papayas, halved, deseeded
   and cut into 1 cm/½ inch dice**

½ small red chilli, finely chopped

2 spring onions, finely sliced

**1 tablespoon finely chopped
   coriander**

sea salt and pepper

2 Combine the lime juice, olive oil and balsamic vinegar in a bowl. Add the papayas, chilli, spring onions and diced red peppers and toss gently until combined. Season to taste with salt and pepper and stir in the coriander. Cover and chill in the refrigerator for about 30 minutes before serving to allow the flavours to blend and develop. Best eaten on the same day.

This sweet, tangy salsa is inviting to look at and refreshing to eat. Serve with Griddled Red Snapper (see page 78) or with grilled and fried meat, chicken and vegetables.

sweet and hot
dipping sauce

2	Serves
10 minutes	Preparation time
2 minutes	Cooking time
65	Kcal
275	KJ
1 g	Protein
2 g	Fat
12 g	CHO

1 Slice the cucumber into matchsticks without peeling. Slice the chillies into thin rounds and mix them with the cucumber in a serving bowl.

1 cucumber

2 small red chillies, seeded

2 tablespoons sugar

4 tablespoons white wine vinegar
   or rice vinegar

1 tablespoon water

1 tablespoon roughly chopped
   roasted peanuts

sea salt

coriander leaves, to garnish

2 Mix together the sugar, vinegar and water in a small saucepan and season with salt. Heat to dissolve the sugar. Cool, pour over the cucumber mixture. Stir in the peanuts, garnish with the coriander and serve.

This pretty dip, or cucumber pickle, comes from Indonesia. It can be served with seafood or chicken brochettes, satays and Thai fish and Prawn cakes (see page 97), to add a fiery kick.

savoury salsa

Serves	**250** ml/8 fl oz
Preparation time	**10** minutes
Kcal	**130**
KJ	**536**
Protein	**1** g
Fat	**14** g
CHO	**1** g

6 tablespoons finely chopped flat
leaf parsley

3 tablespoons finely chopped basil

2 garlic cloves, crushed

1 tablespoon finely chopped
gherkin

2 anchovy fillets, rinsed and finely
chopped

1 teaspoon Dijon mustard

150 ml/¼ pint olive oil

1–3 tablespoons orange or lime
juice

pepper

1 Combine the parsley, basil,
garlic, gherkin, anchovies and
mustard in a bowl. Whisk in the oil
and add the orange or lime juice.

2 Transfer the salsa to a screw-
top jar and store in the refrigerator
for up to 1 week.

This rich sauce is perfect with boiled artichokes, griddled vegetables or steak. It can also be
tossed with warm pasta or new potatoes.

citrus dressing

about **200** ml/**7** fl oz | Makes
10 minutes | Preparation time
819 | Kcal
3369 | KJ
1 g | Protein
88 g | Fat
6 g | CHO

2 teaspoons Dijon mustard

1 teaspoon sugar

juice of 1 lemon

2 tablespoons white wine vinegar

8 tablespoons olive oil

pinch of sea salt

generous grinding of black pepper

1 Put all the ingredients into a screw-top jar and shake vigorously until well combined. Alternatively, place all the ingredients in a small bowl and whisk with a fork.

Serve this tangy dressing with Griddled Scallops (see page 82) or as an alternative dressing for Griddled Rainbow Trout (see page 93).

desserts

Griddled fruit is the perfect way to end a meal. Warm, aromatic and luscious, serve on its own as a healthy and light finale or with ice cream and a variety of toppings.

pineapple
with rumbled mascarpone

Serves	**4**
Preparation time	**5** minutes
Preparation time	about **10** minutes
Kcal	**332**
KJ	**1383**
Protein	**7** g
Fat	**24** g
CHO	**21** g

1 Heat the griddle pan. Put on the pineapple slices and cook for about 2 minutes on each side.

2 Mix the mascarpone, rum and brown sugar together. Serve the griddled pineapple with the rumbled mascarpone spooned over the top.

**1 golden Cape pineapple, peeled
   and sliced**

6 tablespoons mascarpone cheese

2 tablespoons rum

2 tablespoons fine brown sugar

Pineapple will continue to ripen even after it is picked. Select one that has a fragrant scent and an even colouring.

oranges
with rosewater and cinnamon

4	Serves
5 minutes	Preparation time
about **15** minutes	Cooking time
157	Kcal
668	KJ
2 g	Protein
0 g	Fat
39 g	CHO

4 oranges

4 tablespoons rosewater

4 teaspoons cinnamon

4 tablespoons muscovado sugar

1 Heat the griddle pan. Slice each of the oranges into 5 circles. Place on the hot griddle in batches and sprinkle with the rosewater, cinnamon and sugar. Cook for 2 minutes on each side.

2 Carefully transfer the oranges to individual serving bowls and pour over the juices from the griddle pan. Serve immediately or leave to cool a little.

Rosewater is made from distilled rose petals and is often used to flavour Middle Eastern and Indian desserts.

bananas
with chocolate and honey

Serves	**4**
Preparation time	**5** minutes
Cooking time	**10** minutes
Kcal	**385**
KJ	**1624**
Protein	**4** g
Fat	**12** g
CHO	**70** g

4 ripe bananas

75 g/3 oz good-quality dark chocolate

75 g/3 oz white chocolate

4 tablespoons runny honey

1 Heat the griddle pan. Place the bananas, still in their skins, on the griddle and cook, turning constantly, for 10 minutes, by which time the skins will have gone black.

2 Grate the dark and white chocolate and mix together.

3 When the bananas have cooled a little, peel them and cut them in half lengthways. Drizzle the honey along the length, and sprinkle with the grated chocolate.

These delicious bananas can also be cooked on a barbecue, an ideal dessert for warm summer evenings.

plum and mascarpone
bruschetta

4	Serves
10 minutes	Preparation time
10 minutes	Cooking time
418	Kcal
1753	KJ
13 g	Protein
20 g	Fat
49 g	CHO

1 Heat the griddle pan to very hot. Slice the ciabatta in half and then slice again horizontally into 4 pieces. Toast the cut side on the griddle. Place the toasted ciabatta on serving plates and spread with the mascarpone.

1 ciabatta

200 g/7 oz mascarpone cheese

8 ripe plums, stoned and quartered, or figs, apricots or peaches

4 tablespoons sweet dessert wine

few basil leaves, to decorate

2 Place the plums on the griddle and cook for 4 minutes, turning occasionally. Add the dessert wine to the pan, stir and cook for about 30 seconds, then spoon the plums on to the ciabatta toasts. Decorate with basil leaves and serve immediately.

Damsons are very good cooking plums and are frequently used for jams and pies. Often plums have bitter-tasting skins which make a wonderful contrast to the juicy flesh, sweet wine and mascarpone cheese.

griddled figs
with yogurt and honey

Serves	**4**
Preparation time	**5** minutes
Cooking time	**10** minutes
Kcal	**144**
KJ	**610**
Protein	**5** g
Fat	**5** g
CHO	**20** g

8 ripe figs

4 tablespoons Greek yogurt

2 tablespoons clear honey

1 Heat the griddle pan and add the figs. Cook for 8 minutes, turning occasionally, until they are charred on the outside. Remove and cut in half. Arrange the figs on 4 plates and serve with a spoonful of Greek yogurt and honey spooned over the top.

Warm figs with thick, Greek yogurt and honey drizzled over them make a delicious and quick dessert.

warm citrus salad
with lime syrup

4	Serves
20 minutes	Preparation time
about **10** minutes	Cooking time
179	Kcal
760	KJ
2 g	Protein
0 g	Fat
45 g	CHO

1 In a small saucepan, gently dissolve the sugar in the water, then boil for 5 minutes without stirring. As it might splutter, carefully pour all the citrus juices into the sugar syrup and bring it back to the boil, stirring constantly. Remove from the heat and add the lime rind.

4 tablespoons caster sugar

2 tablespoons water

1 pomelo, peeled and segmented, keeping the juices

1 ruby grapefruit, peeled and segmented, keeping the juices

1 pink grapefruit, peeled and segmented, keeping the juices

2 white grapefruits, peeled and segmented, keeping the juices

juice and rind of 2 limes

small bunch of mint, to decorate

2 Heat the griddle pan to very hot and then quickly scorch the citrus segments on both sides. Place the citrus segments in a serving bowl, pour over the syrup and decorate with the mint leaves.

A pomelo is similar to a grapefruit but larger and pear-shaped with a thickish, greeny-yellow skin and membrane. Its flesh is sharp and sweet and less juicy than grapefruit.

panettone
with peaches and clotted cream

Serves	**4**
Preparation time	**5** minutes
Cooking time	about **10** minutes
Kcal	**557**
KJ	**2310**
Protein	**4** g
Fat	**49** g
CHO	**26** g

4 peaches, halved and stoned

4 slices of panettone

ground cinnamon, for dusting

4 tablespoons clotted cream

icing sugar, for dusting

1 Heat the griddle pan and cook the peaches on each side until slightly charred, about 5 minutes. Set aside.

2 Lightly toast the panettone for 1–2 minutes on each side.

3 Place the peaches on the panettone and dust with cinnamon. Spoon over the clotted cream, dust with icing sugar and serve immediately.

The textures and colours of this dessert look so inviting. Griddled panettone is delicious, and other fruits, such as apples, apricots and pears, can be griddled and used instead of the peaches.

hot mango
and coconut with ginger cream

4	Serves
15 minutes	Preparation time
about **5** minutes	Cooking time
605	Kcal
2509	KJ
4 g	Protein
54 g	Fat
29 g	CHO

1 Melt the butter in the griddle pan over a gentle heat. Scatter the coconut on a plate and firmly press the mango slices into the coconut until they are covered on both sides. Place the mango slices on the griddle and cook for 2 minutes on each side, or until the coconut is lightly toasted.

50 g/2 oz unsalted butter

1 fresh coconut, flesh grated, or

125 g/4 oz desiccated coconut

4 mangoes, peeled and sliced

2 To make the ginger cream, fold the ginger slices and syrup into the double cream and serve with the hot, crispy mango slices.

ginger cream:

4 pieces of bottled stem ginger,

sliced, and 2 tablespoons syrup

from the jar

250 ml/8 fl oz double cream, lightly

whipped

To crack a coconut, carefully hold the coconut in one hand and pierce 2 of the eyes with a skewer. Pour the water into a small bowl and reserve for another use. Using a hammer, hit the coconut all around the centre, then pull open the 2 halves. Break up the halves and grate the flesh.

honeyed peaches

Serves **4**

Preparation time **15** minutes

Cooking time about **15** minutes

Kcal **303**

KJ **1276**

Protein **2** g

Fat **7** g

CHO **41** g

1 Cut a small cross in the top and bottom of each peach and place them in a pan of boiling water. Leave for 20 seconds and transfer with a slotted spoon to a bowl of cold water. Peel, cut in half lengthways and remove the stone.

2 Place the Marsala, honey and orange rind in a small saucepan, bring to the boil, then simmer for 2 minutes. Add the peach halves and simmer for 3–4 minutes until just tender. Remove the pan from the heat and leave the peaches to cool in the syrup.

3 Remove the peaches with a slotted spoon and bring the remaining syrup to the boil and boil until reduced by half.

4 Heat the griddle pan. Brush the peaches with the melted butter and place on the griddle and cook on each each side until slightly charred, about 5 minutes.

5 Transfer the hot peaches to serving bowls, spoon over a little of the syrup and crumble over the amaretti biscuits. Serve with vanilla ice cream or crème fraîche, if liked.

4 ripe peaches

300 ml/½ pint Marsala

4 tablespoons clear honey

1 strip of orange rind

25 g/1 oz butter, melted

4 amaretti biscuits

vanilla ice cream or crème

  fraîche, to serve (optional)

Sweet fragrant peaches served hot from the griddle with a Marsala flavoured syrup and crunchy amaretti biscuits make a simple but spectacular dessert. Use very ripe peaches as they have the best flavour.

caramelized apples

with flamed calvados

4	Serves
5 minutes	Preparation time
about **15** minutes	Cooking time
264	Kcal
1104	KJ
1 g	Protein
12 g	Fat
33 g	CHO

60 g/2½ oz butter

4 tablespoons caster sugar

4 dessert apples, cored and sliced

4 tablespoons Calvados

crème fraîche, to serve (optional)

1 Heat the griddle pan and gently melt the butter with the sugar. When it is syrupy, add the apple slices and cook, stirring occasionally, for about 5 minutes, until they are tender against the point of a knife.

2 Turn the heat up until the apples are golden and the syrup is thick and brown. Pour in the Calvados and carefully flame to burn off the alcohol. Serve immediately with a large spoonful of crème fraîche, if liked.

Calavados is the famed brandy made by distilling cider, a very old tradition in Normandy, France. It makes a lovely companion to apples and can also be found in other Norman specialities.

figs
with blackberries on toast

Serves	**4**
Preparation time	**5–10** minutes
Cooking time	**8–10** minutes
Kcal	**236** (not including fromage frais or yogurt)
KJ	**1000**
Protein	**5** g
Fat	**6** g
CHO	**41** g

12 ripe figs

125 g/4 oz blackberries

pared rind and juice of 2 oranges

2 tablespoons crème de cassis

1 tablespoon caster sugar

½ teaspoon cinnamon

25 g/1 oz butter, melted

4 slices brioche or white bread

**fromage frais or Greek yogurt, to
serve (optional)**

1 Cut the figs into quarters, slicing almost, but not all the way through, so that the quarters fall back like flower petals. Cut out 4 squares of double-thickness foil and place 3 figs and a quarter of the blackberries on each piece.

2 Cut the orange rind into julienne strips. Place in a bowl, stir in the orange juice and the crème de cassis and divide between the fig parcels. Bring up the edges of the foil and press to seal.

3 Mix the sugar, cinnamon and melted butter in a bowl and brush over one side of each brioche or bread slice.

4 Cook the fig parcels in a pre-heated oven, 200°C (400°F), Gas Mark 6, for about 8–10 minutes, or until the figs are hot and slightly soft. Towards the end of the cooking time, add the brioche or bread slices to a medium hot griddle pan, with the buttered side up, and toast until golden.

5 Serve the cinnamon toast on individual plates, topped with the figs and blackberries. Add a spoonful of fromage frais or Greek yogurt, if liked.

Hot, squidgy figs and blackberries baked in liqueur are served with crispy cinnamon brioche toast to mop up the delicious cooking juices.

hot pears
with cherry and star anise sauce

4	Serves
10 minutes	Preparation time
about **12** minutes	Cooking time
159	Kcal
670	KJ
1 g	Protein
5 g	Fat
29 g	CHO

1 To make the cherry and star anise sauce, place the cherries and star anise in a saucepan with the cold water and heat gently for 5 minutes. Press through a sieve with the back of a spoon to remove the stones and skins and add honey to sweeten, if needed.

2 Heat the griddle pan. Place the pears on the griddle, cut-side down, and cook for 2–3 minutes. Baste with the butter and honey, then turn over and cook for a further 2–3 minutes. Place the griddled pears in serving bowls, drizzle with honey and serve with vanilla ice cream, if liked.

4 pears, halved and cored

25 g/1 oz butter, melted

1 tablespoon clear honey

vanilla ice cream, to serve
   (optional)

cherry and star anise sauce:

250 g/8 oz fresh, ripe cherries, or
   canned cherries, drained

2 star anise

2 tablespoons cold water

clear honey, to taste

A melon baller is an excellent tool to use for coring pears.

fruit skewers
with coconut custard

Serves	**4**
Preparation time	**25** minutes, plus chilling
Cooking time	**15–20** minutes
Kcal	**479**
KJ	**2008**
Protein	**6** g
Fat	**24** g
CHO	**60** g

1 kg/2 lb assorted fruits in season
(e.g. mangoes, papayas, peaches,
strawberries, oranges, apples,
pears)

lime or lemon juice, for brushing

2 tablespoons muscovado or caster
sugar

coconut custard:

4 egg yolks

75 g/3 oz caster sugar

150 ml/¼ pint coconut milk

150 ml/¼ pint double cream

1 tablespoon rum or Cointreau
(optional)

1 First make the coconut custard. Whisk the egg yolks and sugar in a bowl until thick and creamy. Mix the coconut milk and cream in a saucepan and heat to just below boiling point, then pour into the beaten egg yolk mixture, whisking constantly. Return to a clean pan. Place over a low heat and stir constantly until the mixture coats the back of a spoon. Do not let the mixture boil or the custard will curdle. Remove the pan from the heat and strain the custard into a bowl. Stir in the rum or Cointreau, if using, and cover. When cool, chill the custard in the refrigerator.

2 Heat the griddle pan. Prepare the fruit and cut it into even-sized pieces. Brush with lime or lemon juice and cook on the griddle pan for 2–3 minutes on each side, then sprinkle the fruit with the sugar and cook for 1 further minute. Thread the fruit on to 8 skewers, alternating the colours, or serve in individual bowls. Serve the custard in a separate bowl for dipping, like a cold fondue.

The coconut custard also makes a delicious accompaniment to hot puddings, such as a chocolate bread and butter pudding.

melon
and rosewater granita

4	Serves
10 minutes, plus freezing	Preparation time
about **5** minutes	Cooking time
112	Kcal
477	KJ
1 g	Protein
0 g	Fat
28 g	CHO

2 Charentais or rock melons

75 g/3 oz caster sugar

175 ml/6 fl oz water

½ teaspoon rosewater

fromage frais, to serve (optional)

1 Cut the melons in half, remove the seeds and scoop out the flesh into a food processor or blender.

2 Place the sugar and water in a small saucepan and heat for about 1–2 minutes until the sugar has dissolved. Increase the heat and boil for another 2 minutes without stirring, then remove from the heat and leave to cool slightly.

3 Add half of the sugar syrup to the melon flesh and blend until smooth. Pour into a bowl and stir in the rosewater and more sugar syrup to taste; the amount needed will depend on the sweetness of the fruit.

4 Pour the melon mixture into a 25 x 15 cm/10 x 6 inch tin and chill in the refrigerator. When the mixture is quite cold, transfer the tin to the freezer for 1 hour or until ice crystals have formed around the rim and the mixture is starting to freeze on the base. Stir the mixture thoroughly with a fork, then replace in the freezer. Repeat every 45 minutes until uniform crystals have formed. This will take about 4–5 hours. Serve at once or within 4–6 hours. To serve, spoon into glasses and top with fromage frais, if liked.

A fresh icy granita is perfect as a light dessert after a rich main dish, or served between courses to clear the palate. Although this granita takes time, it is quite easy to make. Serve with Warm Citrus Salad (see page 129).

glossary

almonds – are available in two types, sweet and bitter and can be bought whole, ground, chopped, flaked and blanched. Almonds have a higher protein content than most nuts and a high content of fats and calcium.

asparagus – is a member of the lily family; green and white are the two main types of the many varieties. When buying fresh, look for equal-sized spears with closed tips, smooth texture and non-woody stems.

avocados – are best bought a few days before use, but ripening can be hastened by storing in a brown paper bag with a banana. Cut avocados can be brushed with lemon juice to prevent discolouration.

balsamic vinegar – is made in Modena, Italy. The grape juice is aged in wooden barrels for around seven years. The longer it has to mature, the deeper and sweeter the flavour – and steeper the price. It can be used to deglaze pans for gravy, and to dress berries and salads.

basil – is perhaps the best-known Italian herb. Pesto could not be made without these soft, green and flavoursome leaves. Purple basil has a more delicate flavour and makes a beautiful garnish.

bay leaves – are most often used dried or as part of a bouquet garni.

butternut squash – is one of the most popular and easily available winter squashes. It has a large, flat-bottomed pear shape with smooth yellowish skin and firm, nutty-tasting flesh.

capers – are sharp-tasting, pungent buds used to flavour sauces, salads and fish dishes. Capers originate in Mediterranean countries and are usually bottled in brine and should be rinsed in water before using. As a general rule, the smaller they are, the better they taste.

cranberries – are low in fat, high in dietary fibre and rich in vitamin C. Fresh cranberries will keep for about 4 weeks refrigerated in an unopened bag or for up to 10 days once opened.

crème fraîche – is a type of cream that has been treated to sour slightly in order to develop a piquant tang. It is used as a substitute for soured cream.

fennel – is a beautifully shaped vegetable with an aniseed flavour. It is often served with fish and is a good vegetable to use when making kebabs. The delicate fronds make a lovely garnish.

garlic – is a pungent herb much used in French and Italian dishes. A quick method of removing the skin is to crush the clove with the side of a knife and then it can be easily chopped.

juniper berries – are dried berries from the evergreen juniper bush. They can be used in sauces, marinades and crushed as a coating for griddled meats.

leeks – are members of the onion family which have a mild and sweet flavour once cooked. They can be eaten on their own or used in savoury dishes.

mascarpone cheese – is a soft and creamy Italian cheese made from cows' milk and can be used for sweet dishes, such as tiramisu, and savoury dishes.

mooli – is a long, white, tube-shaped vegetable of the radish family. Its flavour is not as strong as ordinary red radishes, which can be substituted if mooli is not available. Mooli is often used in Indian and other Asian cuisines.

nasturtium – are any of various edible plants with yellow, red and orange flowers and round leaves. All parts of the plant may be eaten, except for the root.

olive oil – is available as extra virgin, virgin or just olive oil depending on the way the oil has been extracted, which can greatly alter the taste. Good quality extra virgin olive oil can be expensive, so use a less expensive oil for frying.

olives – are small tree fruits that ripen from green to black. If possible, buy them loose rather than in bottles or cans as these will have the best flavour.

panettone – is an Italian yeast cake enhanced with raisins and candied peel and traditionally served around Christmas.

parma ham – is a famed cured ham from the Parma region of northern Italy. The skin is rubbed in salt then the ham is left to mature for nearly 1 year. It should always be served thinly sliced.

parmesan cheese – is a very well-known, strong, hard cheese made from partially skimmed cows' milk and aged for up to two years. The top quality Parmesan cheese has Parmigiano-Reggiano stamped into the rind. If possible, buy it in a block and grate it as required.

parsnip – is a root vegetable which grows as a tapering, conical root, with green foliage growing above ground. Sizes and tastes do vary – the more mature a parsnip is, the sweeter the taste.

pecorino cheese – is an Italian ewes' milk cheese which is available soft or hard, depending on its age, and in a variety of flavours, depending on its origin. It can be used for grating like Parmesan cheese.

pine nuts – are small, soft oily textured nuts which come from the Mediterranean stone pine tree. Also known as pine kernels, they do not keep for very long and are best kept stored in a refrigerator.

polenta – is a vitamin rich variety of ground maize mixed with water and moulded into a flat golden loaf or served in a softer form. The taste is quite bland so polenta is often combined with other foods.

radicchio – are slightly bitter-tasting red and white leaves that are a variety of chicory. Often sold packaged with other mixed salad leaves, they will keep for a couple of days if refrigerated.

red mullet – has a taste similar to sole. It works well with strong flavours such as garlic and rosemary and is best served griddled, grilled or baked.

red split lentils – do not require soaking and become tender within about 20 minutes of cooking.

rice sticks – vary in size and shape depending on their country of origin. If they are not available, use another type of rice noodle or vermicelli pasta.

ricotta cheese – is a fresh, soft and bland-tasting cheese which should only be used when very fresh. Most commonly used as a base in fillings and paired with spinach in pasta dishes.

rosemary – is a herb widely used in Italy, especially with chicken and lamb. It has a strong aroma and a distinctive taste. The long, spiky green leaves lend attractive texture to dishes if used as a garnish.

sea salt – contain no additives and the crystal shapes of the sea salt flakes or tiny chunks make attractive garnishes on many dishes.

sherry vinegar – has a smooth, rich and slightly tart flavour that blends well with nut oils to make a flavoursome vinaigrette.

spinach – is a leafy, green vegetable which contains more protein than most vegetables.

star anise – has a strong smell of liquorice mixed with aniseed. It may be removed from dishes before serving or left as a decorative garnish.

sun-dried tomatoes – are available dried or bottled in oil. The drying process creates an intensely sweet flavour and a leathery texture.

tarragon vinegar – is a necessary ingredient for making many sauces and is delicious in marinades for chicken, fish and seafood.

tilapia – is a small African fish which can live in both salt and fresh water. The flesh is white and tender and has a sweet flavour. It is available in a variety of colours, whole or in fillets, year round from large supermarkets and fishmongers.

venison – has a strong yet subtle flavour somewhat like a cross between lamb and beef. It blends perfectly with the sharp, sweet taste of cranberries and oranges, and herbs and spices such as rosemary thyme, juniper and cloves.

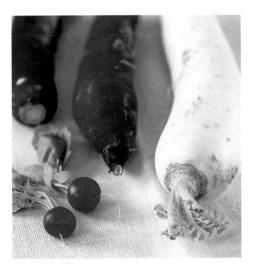

walnuts – have a high calorific content, but are rich in protein and fats and a good source of vitamins B and D, so are important in vegetarian diets.

wasabi – is sometimes called Japanese horseradish as it has similar potent qualities. Wasabi paste is available in tubes and is often served with sushi.

watercress – is a small, dark green plant with peppery-tasting leaves and stems. Rich in calcium and vitamins A and C, it is often used as a garnish or an addition to salads and soups.

yeast extract – is an important ingredient in a vegetarian or vegan diet as it is a good source of B complex vitamins and provides iron, calcium and flavour to foods.

Index

Acknowledgements

Octopus Publishing Group Ltd. / Gus Filgate 25 / Graham Kirk 27, 114, 116 / **Sandra Lane** 6, 7, 19, 28, 29, 35, 46, 97, 101, 103, 111, 113, 115, 119, 125, 129, 131, 135, 138, 139, 140, 141 / **David Loftus** 31, 33, 52, 84 / **James Merrell** 5, 122-123, 132, 134, 137 / **Hilary Moore** 8, 11, 14, 21 / **Simon Smith** 68 / **Ian Wallace** Front Cover, Back Cover, Endpapers, 121 / **Philip Webb** 12-13, 15, 16, 17, 18, 20, 22, 24, 30, 36-37, 38, 40, 42, 45, 47, 48, 50, 54, 56-57, 58, 60, 62, 66, 67, 69, 70, 72, 73, 74, 76-77, 78, 80, 82, 83, 85, 86, 87, 88, 90, 92, 93, 94, 96, 98-99, 100, 102, 104, 107, 124, 128, 130